100 Secrets
to
Creative
Leadership

Michael "Mitch" Droske

CREATIVE LEADERSHIP CAFE, LLC
Anthem, AZ

DEDICATION

To my wife, Ruby—

You're my co-conspirator in these crazy adventures of life. Thanks for inspiring me to dip my toes back into the leadership landscape to help yet another generation of people on their journey to the greatest versions of themselves.

With deep love and appreciation for who you are and what you mean to me,

Mitch

ACKNOWLEDGEMENTS

I would like to thank the following people who have unknowingly contributed to this book in one way or another:

- My Dad, my hero. I miss you. I see you in these pages.

- Bob Brown for being a great mentor and friend.

- Robert "Bubba" Sanders for teaching me how to lead.

- Larry Hogan Sr. for caring enough to lead me well.

- The United States Air Force for training and discipline.

- Orville and Wilbur Wright—for airplanes.

CONTENTS

100 Secrets to Creative Leadership

PREFACE

We are all born with a love for crayons and building blocks and exploration. We start life with an insane amount of curiosity asking "Why?" in almost every conversation we're in. Unfortunately, our creative nature tends to get stifled by our educational system where gold stars are not handed out if you color outside the lines. We quickly learn through academic classes like algebra and geometry that there is only one correct answer for every problem, and even more so, there is only one correct way to solve for the correct answer. After spending so much time getting jammed into a box, we find ourselves spending the rest of our lives trying to get out of it—that is, of course, except for the creative types who buck the system because they have an unbridled desire to freely explore beyond the boundaries of the "acceptable."

This book showcases 100 carefully selected words which are critical to success in business and in life for people who are leaders or are aspiring to be one. Many people hold the title, but few people actually lead. You see, the definition of leadership is simple: "It's the art of influence." If you don't have people willingly following you, you aren't influencing them. "Creative" leadership takes things a bit further. The creative leader encourages free thinking, imagination, deep innovation and insane amounts of curiosity. The creative leader takes us back to our childhood where making things from nothing was commonplace, and breaking the rules on what is and is not possible happened every day. This book can be consumed in any way you want. Let your needs drive your consumption. Start at the back; start in the middle. Read it from cover to cover, or pick a word daily which has special significance to you. You decide. Each story should kindle the flames of your imagination, and each "secret" should get you thinking of ways to do things differently. There is no right or wrong with this book. Let it shape you and the people you lead in the most unique and special ways.

"Creativity is allowing yourself to make mistakes. Art is knowing which ones to keep."

Scott Adams

SECRET #1

HUMILITY

hu·mil·i·ty (hū-mil'-ə-tee)

1. the belief that you are not superior to, or better than, others.
2. humbleness.

HUMILITY

When US Airways Flight 1549 struck a flock of geese while departing LaGuardia Airport in New York City, the powerful engines quickly became disabled, and the crew was forced to ditch the multi-million dollar jet in the Hudson River.

The captain, Chelsea "Sully" Sullenberger, led his team in an expert landing and subsequent rescue that was quickly deemed "The Miracle on the Hudson." Hailed as a hero on nearly every television network around the globe, a humble Sully offered a different way of thinking about the outcome. "One way of looking at this might be that for 42 years I've been making small, regular deposits in the bank of experience, education and training. And on January 15th, the balance was sufficient so that I could make a very large withdrawal."

Captain Sullenberger could have boasted, but he chose to be humble. He was quick to deflect the praise leveled at him and instead highlighted the strengths of those around him. He realized his newsworthy accomplishment was merely a byproduct of the great training he received over a lengthy career.

SECRET #1 to Creative Leadership:
The creative leader is gentle but not weak. People flock to be around these caring mentors. They exude strength and confidence without being arrogant or cocky. They always take the "road less traveled"—the one called Humility Lane.

They take risks by sharing new ideas which could subject themselves and their work to public critique. They also know they will sometimes receive accolades for their unique ideas, and they willingly accept it, but they don't linger on praise. They stay grounded. They know not every idea is a winner.

SECRET #2

FORM

form   (fourm)

1. the shape of someone or something.
2. a pattern or mold.
3. the manner by which something is produced or conducted.

FORM

The Sensei of my karate class was obsessed with form. I, however, had none. My form was so bad, it seemed my limbs were pre-destined to do nothing but chaotically fly around like plastic furniture in a hurricane. My sensei wasn't very patient, and I got yelled at—a lot.

Like my crazed sensei, most people seem obsessed by form. Pick up almost any magazine, and it will prove my point. In it, you'll find countless curvaceous models whose attractive lines have us striving to duplicate the results they have achieved, even though in most cases, it is neither reasonable nor realistic.

Whether it's about karate, beach bodies, public speaking, ballet, novels, orchestras or calligraphy, *form* has one common thread—discipline. For without discipline, form seems to lack beauty. The question is, I suppose, are we chasing the beauty or the discipline which produces it?

SECRET #2 to Creative Leadership:
Creative leaders spend a lot of time working with their teams to develop self-discipline. They know that the discipline will initially come from them, and then at some point, it will come from their employees. They MODEL consistency, and they EXPECT consistency in return. They don't just try to "slap lipstick on a pig" and hope to make it pretty. The pig won't care, and everyone else still sees just a pig.

CLs know dance shoes don't make the dancer; paint brushes don't make the painter; keyboards don't make the writer; fish-bone diagrams don't make the problem-solver. Creative leaders know that true *form* comes from the way each person creatively gets the tools to do what she wants them to do. A masterpiece only becomes so in the hands of the master, and a master only becomes so through training and discipline.

SECRET #3

RESILIENCE

re·sil·ience (rə-zill'-yuhns)

1. the ability to bounce back or return to original form or shape after being stressed, compressed, stretched, etc.
2. the ability to get back to a successful state after enduring a difficult situation.

RESILIENCE

There are a few creatures in this world that I really, really hate—snakes, scorpions and sharks.

I'm guessing Bethany Hamilton also hates sharks. The 23-year old had her left arm severed just below the shoulder by a tiger shark while she was surfing the waves at Tunnels Beach in Kauai. Despite losing 60% of her blood volume and staring death squarely in the face, Bethany survived. As amazing as that is, the most remarkable portion of her story unfolded thereafter.

Within one month of her devastating injury, she was not only back in the water, she was back surfing again in the very waters where that ocean predator took her arm—which, incidentally, was one of her primary tools she used to balance herself on the surfboard.

Hey, I watched the movie *Jaws*, and that was enough to keep me from going beyond knee-deep ocean water for the rest of my life. Bethany, however, is not one to be deterred. With incredible resilience, she was able to master surfing again, and in just three short months was back competing professionally.

SECRET #3 to Creative Leadership:
Creative leaders take calculated risks knowing that failure will visit them at some point—it is inevitable. They do their best to approach those setbacks in the same way Bethany would tackle them. When they "get bucked off a horse," they get back on. Does it hurt? Probably. But does their resilience pay off? Definitely. It is important to note that a CL will not simply jump back into a situation and do things the same way they did when they were unsuccessful. Instead, they evaluate, make small changes, and they track the effect of those changes. CLs know there is an untapped resilience in everyone. They strive to find and foster that resilience so people essentially become impervious to setbacks.

SECRET #4

FOCUS

fo·cus (fō-kəs)

1. a clear object of attention.
2. an ability to set aside all distractions.
3. to capture something visually with precise sharpness and clarity.

FOCUS

On April 8th in 2009, Somali pirates hijacked the Maersk Alabama, a cargo vessel operating under the US flag. After stealing a significant sum of money, they then kidnapped the captain and took him with them while attempting to flee by lifeboat.

Sharpshooters from Navy Seal Team Six were dispatched to assist and arrived on Friday, April 10th. For several days, three marksmen of the Seal team were positioned on vessels nearby at various different angles in anticipation of an order from the President of the United States to eliminate the threat by killing the pirates.

Despite the unrelenting ocean waves constantly pitching and rolling the decks of both the lifeboat and the vessels hosting the ever-patient Seals, each marksman kept their moving target in their gun sights the entire time—for three straight days. When the order finally came, they were ready.

How focused are you? How sharp and directed is your attention? Are you easily distracted, or can you "dial in"?

SECRET #4 to Creative Leadership:
A lack of focus can have you floundering around, but hyper-focusing on any one thing can lead you to miss other critical things happening around you. Creative leaders operate somewhere in the middle where balance tends to prevent the extremes. But what is really interesting about CLs is that they sometimes force themselves NOT to focus—at least on things they already know and solutions they've already used at other companies or in other situations. They gather raw data from everywhere, without initially evaluating it, and then, and only then, do they dial in their thoughts to create a UNIQUE outcome. It's like taking a portrait photo with an iPhone. In the end, only one thing is in focus—everything else is blurry. Result: The focus is on the right thing.

SECRET #5

IDENTITY

iden·ti·ty (ī-dən-tə-tee)

1. that which makes you who you are.

IDENTITY

Your identity is so much more than the combination of your social security number, driver's license, date of birth and physical address. In fact, your true identity has nothing to do with information which can be stolen. Furthermore, your identity is not found in the roles you fill (e.g. brother, son, mother, aunt), and it's not found in the jobs you have done or the titles you've held. It also can't be found in your successes or failures, in the possessions you've acquired or lost, or in the relationships you've grown or damaged.

Sadly though, many people live their entire lives attempting to fulfill man-made expectations of who they should be, and they measure their self-worth through the judgmental eyes of people who have no better understanding of personal identity than they do. Some of the most lost and confused people I know have everything by worldly standards, and yet they are empty inside searching for their life's purpose and meaning.

Whether you know it or not, you are a unique masterpiece created by God—you're the only one like you in the entire world. Your true identity can only be found by connecting yourself to the Creator. "Listen" to what He says about you.

SECRET #5 to Creative Leadership:
Creative leaders recognize the power of individuality and the diversity of thought. They want people to be who they were created to be. CLs recognize that everyone is on a journey through this life, and they know most people have been wounded along the way. When they see someone struggling with identity issues, they lean in and ask questions to find out when or where they lost it. It's in that backwards journey where people can often discover their true, unique selves.

SECRET #6

TEACHABILITY

teach·able   (tee-chə-bəl)

1. demonstrated willingness and ability to learn.

TEACHABILITY

Until the day you draw your last breath, you are a work in progress. You never stop learning—EVER.

One of the best qualities you can have is teachability. Peyton Manning, former NFL quarterback of the Denver Broncos, is arguably one of the greatest quarterbacks to ever play the game. Interestingly, his most admirable skill is not found in his on-field execution—it's his teach-ability which is widely hailed as the greatest determiner of his success.

Hey, it's easy to be teachable when you know little about what people are telling you. The real challenge, however, comes when you have significant understanding of how something works (or should work) but purposefully position yourself to have your thinking challenged and your decisions questioned by everyone—even those who might have less experience than you do. Manning always positioned himself to be in learning mode. He remained teachable.

SECRET #6 to Creative Leadership:
A creative leader typically has a GOOD answer to almost every problem but knows that someone else might have a SPECTACULAR idea which must be considered. CLs know their greatest strength is not found in how much THEY know but rather in their ability to find solutions regardless of the source from which they come. The don't let pride close their minds or the door to an opportunity. Creative leaders always stretch themselves by researching things they don't know; trying things they can't currently do; and pushing themselves beyond their current capabilities. Teachability is a core characteristic of a CL. It requires a level of vulnerability that is very uncomfortable for most people, but it is the sturdy foundation upon which true greatness is achieved.

SECRET #7

DETERMINATION

de·ter·mi·na·tion (dih-tur-mə-nā'-shun)

1. the unrelenting drive to press forward through something difficult despite obstacles or barriers in your way.

DETERMINATION

When I think about determination, I think about Helen Keller, the famed American author, activist and lecturer who was the first deaf-blind person to earn a Bachelor of Arts degree—and she would go on to transform the hearts and minds of the world through her selfless acts of human kindness. Helen was a textbook example of determination.

Why is it some people have such an incorruptible, laser-like determination when it comes to approaching tasks, while others find it difficult to consider investing themselves in anything for more than a very brief period of time? Well, the answer probably lies somewhere between the way we are individually wired and personal choice.

Consider the procrastinator who has been avoiding a project with a fast-approaching deadline. Can't seem to focus. But, when crunch-time is upon him, suddenly determination shows its face. Why not show determination right out of the gate? Why wait? Just get it done. The point is that most people can control their level of determination when they take the time to count the costs. If you act early and with great amounts of determination, think of how much you could do.

SECRET #7 to Creative Leadership:
If your level of determination doesn't match those with whom you're working, take time to count the costs together, and give each other reasons to stay engaged. Creative leaders aren't robots—they, too, must fight the urge to delay tasks until they "feel" like doing them. The big difference is that a creative leader will find someone whose determination level is high, and then they will draw from it. CLs also know that creating can be messy, and messy can look like a lack of progress. They accept the mess but insist on forward movement.

SECRET #8

INTEGRITY

in·teg·ri·ty (in-tɔg'-rə-tee)

1. having a character of honesty and impartiality
2. soundness; without compromise; complete or whole

INTEGRITY

True integrity is tough to find modeled these days. There has been such a fast-moving erosion of moral character in our society in the past decade or so, you might easily find yourself surrounded by people who do the right thing only when someone is watching. Maybe not even then.

Interestingly, research shows we all highly value integrity. So, basically, there is a widespread double-standard on this issue. Consider this: What if your bank only did the right thing when someone was watching? What if your doctor or pharmacist was the same way? Would you still use them? Doubtful.

Are you a person of integrity? Do you do the right thing all the time even if it sometimes hurts? As I said earlier, we are all a work in progress, so if you screw up, recognize it, make good on the situation, and determine to do better next time. Before long, you'll find you are doing the right thing all the time. And the best part about it is that you no longer have to live with the regret of bad choices. Furthermore, when you are honest all the time, you don't have to try to remember which lie you told to which person. That can be exhausting.

SECRET #8 to Creative Leadership:
Creative leaders don't expect more from the people they lead than what they demonstrate through their own examples. CLs know that a high level of integrity will ultimately breed integrity. People typically follow the leader. Also, as CLs lead, they are aware that integrity also has to do with refusing to compromise their style as they seek to blend their efforts with those of the people with which they interact. It is vitally important to be true to yourself and your unique style. CLs don't hold back in sharing their ideas, but they also don't overwhelm the conversation and quiet others with a forceful, heavy-handed approach. CLs are true to themselves, and they support all others around them in doing the same.

17

SECRET #9

CHARISMA

cha·ris·ma (kuh-riz'-muh)

1. a quality in a person that draws others; a sometimes unexplainable appeal or charm.
2. an informal power or influence over others.

CHARISMA

Charismatic leaders are found in all environments. We find them in the White House, in church pulpits, in gangs, and in corporations across the globe. Charismatic leaders are like magnets to the people who follow them—and not necessarily because of the knowledge they possess or the position they hold but rather because of an almost unexplainable trait—the "it" factor. Whatever "it" is, they have "it". People are drawn to them like flies to a picnic.

Being charismatic is not something you could easily fake if it isn't a part of who you are, so trying to become the magnet you're not might actually *repel* people rather than *compel* them. Having said that, we can always learn to be more outgoing, friendly and approachable even if a party doesn't seem to break out wherever we happen to be standing.

SECRET #9 to Creative Leadership:
Creative leaders may or may not have natural charisma, but they are <u>always</u> mindful of anyone on their team who does. The CL is aware that a charismatic person on the team could either prove to be supportive and tremendously beneficial, or that person could be consciously or unconsciously working against the CL and influencing others to do the same. The CL is quick to identify this charismatic, informal leader and finds ways to gain his support on any new departmental changes so when the message makes it to the "floor", it has positive traction and buy-in almost immediately.

Food for thought: People <u>love</u> to be around creative types because they have a natural curiosity about everything, and they are willing to take risks and "swim against the current." Just be careful they don't become <u>unproductively</u> disruptive and accidently create a coup in your workplace.

SECRET #10

COMPETENCE

com·pe·tent (kahm-pə-tənt)\

1. having adequate or sufficient knowledge, skills, and experience.
2. satisfactory capabilities but not expert.
3. the capacity to function.

COMPETENCE

Nobody likes incompetence, especially if it's found in the person leading your department at work. What's interesting though is that we all expect leaders to be *experts* in everything they oversee, but, in most cases, they are not called to be experts—they are simply called to be competent. And, if you look at the definition of competence, we see it described as "adequate ability" or "the capacity to function." We often expect too much of our leaders, and it actually isn't good for us, or them.

The problem we often get with leaders who are experts at everything is a nasty by-product called micromanagement. It is no mystery that people like to spend energy on things at which they have a gift or talent, so leaders with a strong skill in something tend to over-manage in that area. So be careful of the expectations you place on your leader—it just might come back to haunt you.

SECRET #10 to Creative Leadership:
Creative leaders know that a requirement to have *adequate* ability isn't a free pass to mediocrity for them or the people they lead. CLs never stop improving their capabilities and the way they execute. They are also smart enough to know they must hire strong team members to be the focused   subject matter experts while they keep a firm grip on the *big picture.*

CAUTION: As CLs push themselves to think outside-the-box, they might find it difficult sometimes to adequately express their ideas to others because they aren't always "fully baked" when their excitement about them "forces" them to share—they may not make complete sense to others. In these moments, CLs might come across as incompetent or "flighty." It is important for a CL to slow down, refine their message, and then share. It will be received much better.

SECRET #11

VISION

vi·sion·ary (vi'-zhən-nair-ee)

1. a person who has the ability to imagine what lies ahead.
2. a speculative person who anticipates the future and plans ahead for it.

VISION

If you told me you see things that aren't there, I might be inclined to head to eBay for an exorcism kit. But when it comes to leadership, that's EXACTLY what I want in a leader—someone who sees things that others don't.

Companies need leaders to SEE things that aren't there so they can inspire their teams to create something that doesn't yet exist. They call these people visionaries.

Visionaries rarely just see things in their mind's eye about something they know little about. Instead, they usually have done a lot of research and have given a lot of thought to the situation.

Armed with this information, the typical visionary begins to identify patterns and look for what is, and isn't, there. Then, exercising her imaginative muscles, she methodically explores the world of "What If?" until a ground-breaking idea surfaces with such convincing force it almost produces its own game plan.

Some people might say number-crunching analysts who identify trends upon which to act are visionaries, but I would disagree. I think a visionary is someone who, in the absence of any hard evidence, can still clearly see the direction to proceed as though guided by a giant beacon illuminating the way.

SECRET #11 to Creative Leadership:
Creative leaders have an almost untamed imagination. They never stop contemplating, dreaming, and creating. CLs don't just dabble in things that are familiar or comfortable to them. They live and breathe is a perpetual state of exploration, and they take their employees with them on the journey. CLs know that their best thinking happens in quiet, inspirational spaces where they can let their thoughts run wild. And they journal like crazy to capture whatever travels through their mind during the process. They see everything as useful.

SECRET #12

INSPIRATION

in·spire   \(in-spī´-yur)

1. to spur or instigate with influence.
2. to cause something to take place.

INSPIRATION

When you look at this definition, it can be a little disarming as it introduces the idea of <u>spurring</u> and <u>instigating</u> as the methods used to inspire. While we almost always think of inspirational events as *positive* life-drivers, such harsh sounding methods would suggest that those being inspired are not always willing participants. Oh how true.

PROOF: Think about the power of infomercials. Before you start watching them, you are pretty much fine with your slightly misshapen figure and the 30 or so extra pounds you acquired since high school. Then, they show you those inspirational video testimonials of success stories closely followed by a lot of spurring and instigating to get you to act. Without their spurring, your lack of personal drive would prevent you from responding. By the way, it's the same lack of drive that precipitates the garage sale of that same equipment a year or two later due to lack of use. In most cases, inspiration won't last if the spurring or instigating stops.

SECRET #12 to Creative Leadership:
Spurring and instigating your employees often happens when you assign challenging projects to them that you know will stretch their capabilities, maybe even beyond the point of their imagination. Your support during this time is critical to their success. But that alone might not do it. Consider a typical artist. Jammed up for some reason—unable to produce. And then he creates something amazing. When asked to explain his success, it is inevitable that the word <u>inspiration</u> will surface. Why? Because we sometimes don't know where to start—we need a leap off point. We might be eager but feel unable. Conversely, we might feel able, but we are handcuffed by so many thoughts in our heads that we don't know where to begin. Creative leaders learn to master the <u>mess</u>. They study ways to create connections.

SECRET #13

PASSION

pas·sion·ate (pa'-shuhn-ət)

1. unmistakably strong beliefs, feelings or emotions

PASSION

You probably don't have to go far back in time to recall the last situation you experienced in which you were ruled by intense emotion or strong feelings. I doubt most people would even need to look beyond the present day. Unfortunately, the passion you felt was likely from a negative experience (e.g. cut off in traffic, held up unnecessarily while trying to get coffee, betrayed by someone who took credit for your work, etc.). But when was the last time you were ruled by an intensely good or positive emotion?

What would life be like if you were surrounded by only positive, upbeat people who saw the good even in the bad and felt such strong, positive emotions about their work they could hardly express themselves? One thing is for sure: The average number of sick days would drastically drop.

The challenge is for YOU to be the person who kick-starts this positivity movement in your work center. And once you start the movement, it will be fueled by your passion. Passion to win; passion to help others. Fill YOUR passion tank.

SECRET #13 to Creative Leadership:
Take a good look at your current leadership approach. Are you are fostering a positively passionate working environment or does your style have people scrambling to throw each other under the bus? A creative leader has unrelenting positive beliefs about all people, and she never quits looking for the evidence of it—even in the so called "screw ups" who can't seem to do anything right. The CL doesn't let anything negative rule her. She will, of course, process all of it, but her passion for helping people and achieving great results will guide her thoughts to center around solutions not problems. The CL quickly shifts everyone away from the pain of the problem and dials them into the thing which erases it.

SECRET #14

CONFIDENCE

con·fi·dent (kahn'-fə-dənt)

1. a feeling of solid assurance in the capabilities of someone or something.
2. a strong belief in a particular outcome.

CONFIDENCE

We live in a world where civil wars break out suddenly, businesses rise and fall over a cup of coffee, and economies are anything but stable. As a result, we long for reassurance that everything is going to be okay. In the workplace, we are also desperate to hear those words from our top leaders. We look at their posture, their word choice and their vocal inflection. We look for confidence in them so we can determine if we should be anxious about our employment or calm and assured.

Confidence is an attractive thing. It just *looks good* on a person. From the college kid slam-dunking his first job interview to the President of the United States determinedly addressing the nation in the moments after a terrorist attack, confidence sends the message: "I've got this worked out—rest easy."

In the various different *Rocky* movies about the underdog boxer who always finds a way to come out on top, we are always initially introduced to a Rocky Balboa who obviously lacks confidence—he practically gets killed in the ring, *in every movie*. He looks defeated long before he actually is defeated. But, in every movie, he always comes back with a renewed confidence in his ability—it's what they called "The eye of the tiger." His face always told the story of his confidence level. Does yours?

SECRET #14 to Creative Leadership:
Creative leaders demonstrate confidence—not because they have everything figured out all the time, but because they trust their abilities and the abilities of the people around them. They know the ultimate outcome will be good even if the current picture looks bleak. CLs operate with the "eye of the tiger." They don't accept defeat. They understand that the only time a person can truly be defeated is when he quits. Creative leaders don't quit—ever.

SECRET #15

COMMITMENT

---

com·mit (kə-mit')

1. to purposefully decide to use.
2. to pledge yourself to someone or something.

COMMITMENT

Bacon and eggs. The word commit is about bacon and eggs. Consider the chicken and the pig. For the chicken, the contribution is really nothing more than a donation, but for the pig it is far more—it is a full commitment; a pledge from which there is no return. In poker terms, you might say the pig is "All in."

NBA superstar, Michael Jordan, took the final, game-deciding shot many times in his career and failed. Responding to his critics, he simply said: "You miss 100% of the shots you never take." Jordan knew how to fully commit.

In business we spend too much time in the safe zone like a chicken, offering a donation—a contribution here and there—but not really investing ourselves in the outcome. When was the last time you went "all in"? When was the last time you asked for "the ball" in the final seconds and took a big risk on something at work, literally putting your entire reputation on the line?

SECRET #15 to Creative Leadership:
When you operate from a position of safety, your team is watching you, and it won't be long before no one is taking a risk on anything because they're modeling your conservative approach. Creative leaders play to win; they don't play the game trying not to lose. Remember, Thomas Edison failed—a lot. He also succeeded—a lot. He pledged himself and his efforts to achieving what he set out to do. He didn't waiver when his plans didn't work out. Instead, he stayed committed, learned from each setback, and used it to propel himself forward. Edison was a creative leader. He was the epitome of exploration and influence. Consider how many people have studied his work and have modeled it. He changed the world. You can too. Just focus on being wildly creative and develop your leadership skills so you can influence others along the way.

SECRET #16

GRACE

gra·cious (grās)

1. unmerited generosity and kindness.

GRACE

WIIFM. We live in a world filled with people who always seem to be asking the question: "What's In It For Me?" As a result, people have become consumed with serving their own interests over the interests of others—and the byproduct of this self-centered approach is judgment and condemnation. You see, when everything becomes about you, other people become less important. As they become less important, you tend to critique them more harshly which only serves to elevate you even more. From this pious perch, you can look down at people, and when they struggle with something you can be quick to point it out. Conversely, when they do well at something you can just as quickly downplay it. There is no kindness. There is no grace.

Grace is unmerited favor. In other words, it is kindness without reason. It isn't earned, but it is given anyway.

A few years ago, MMA fighter Mike Pantangco showed the world what grace truly is when he tapped out (a.k.a. quit) during a brutal amateur match against his opponent Jeremy Rasner. Tapouts are common in the MMA but not when you are winning. Yes, Pantangco was winning. In fact, he was brutally beating Rasner. Then suddenly, and without any explanation whatsoever, Pantangco kneeled down and tapped out. Reporters caught up with him later and asked why he would do such a thing. He responded by saying that he did not want to send Rasner to the hospital, so he let him win.

SECRET #16 to Creative Leadership:
I don't know who started it, but many of today's leaders have subscribed to some polluted theory that you need to rule in an authoritative, heavy-handed way. What rubbish! Creative leaders lead with kindness—care, concern and compassion. The extend grace to people. They allow for "do overs." They judge no one harsher than they would judge themselves. They look to serve and not to be served. They lead with love.

SECRET #17

COMPASSION

com·pas·sion \kuhm-pash-uhn\

1. a desire to help those who are in need.

COMPASSION

Years ago, I attended an event by the group Compassion International. During the concert, there was a compelling video about the starving children in Africa who could be helped for a very small monthly contribution. In that moment, my family and I decided to invest in the life of a particular little girl. We did so until we ran into some very pressing financial times—so we stopped sending the money. At first it was hard, but it got easier to ignore her suffering. We just stopped looking at her photo and ignored the monthly mailings we received from CI. We simply looked the other way so we could care for ourselves. How sad.

While I'm pleased to say we've re-engaged with CI and are now sponsoring another child, it makes me sad when I think about how many people in this world can't look past their own needs and help people who are in desperate times enduring unthinkable situations. I've had tough times in my life, but I've never felt all out desperation. Have you? I think it's time we learn to feel for others and take steps to alleviate their suffering. If we don't, the coldness of our hearts might eventually invite our own suffering.

SECRET #17 to Creative Leadership:
Creative leaders have a heart for people, and they take time to show them. CLs get to know the people they work with, and they pay attention to them, looking for any signs that someone might be having a tough day. If they suspect that is true, a CL will quickly engage the person to do a "check-in". They take time to listen if the person wants to talk, and they respectfully understand if the person chooses not to share. But either way, the CL will offer a word of encouragement and will remain watchful in case the bad day gets worse. CLs care. If you want to be a creative leader, get in rhythm with the heartbeat of your people. Then, when something is *off*, you'll feel it almost immediately.

SECRET #18

MOVEMENT

move·ment   (moov-mənt)

1. the process of putting things in motion.
2. gaining ground.

MOVEMENT

A few years ago, when I was working on a project and making no progress whatsoever, a co-worker told me: "Just start moving—in any direction. It's easier to turn a moving car than it is to turn one from a dead stop."

The lesson? You don't have to have it all figured out in order to make progress—any movement whatsoever is beneficial overall. Momentum is what you need.

When I think about movement, I get a picture in my mind of the ballet—graceful, flowing, beautifully choreographed activities perfectly timed to the rhythm of music. Interestingly though, beneath the clean, white tights of every dancer, you would find medical tape supporting various injuries and a host of bruises normally found on a world class boxer. Their hidden "battle damage" is proof of the unrelenting trial and error which has ultimately led to the poetic movements they display when the curtain goes up.

Whether learning to ride a bike, fly a plane, or develop software, it all takes movement. It isn't always pretty, but victory will come—unless you stop moving.

SECRET #18 to Creative Leadership:
Creative leaders insist on movement. In fact, when a CL takes the first steps on a project, he may not even have the direction completely figured out. A CL would rather start moving and risk falling flat on his face than to do nothing at all. At least he would have six feet of forward progress just for trying. And if the fall was in the wrong direction, learning that would be considered forward progress too. So many people don't make a move because they haven't worked out every little detail in their heads about where they are going, what they need to be doing, and exactly how they should be doing it. Ugh! Just move. Once you're in motion, you will feel better, and you can easily make changes and steer in any direction. The initial direction is almost never the final one.

SECRET #19

STRATEGY

stra•te•gy   (stra'-ti-jee)

1. a plan or approach to reach a specified goal or target.

STRATEGY

People often confuse goals and strategy as essentially the same thing, but while interrelated, they <u>are</u> different. Simply put, goals are the "what" and strategy is the "how".

In the Gulf War, General Norman Schwarzkopf had very focused goals—to remove the Iraqi forces from Kuwait and to limit the loss of life in the exchange. The strategies he ultimately developed and deployed were complicated and covert, involving Jason Bourne-like practices certainly worthy of a four-star rating from any movie critic if the events were to be filmed for display on the big screen.

His plans were careful and precise, and they took time to execute—and, as we all know, the U.S. goals were not just met—they were far exceeded. As the General clearly demonstrated, good goals are not enough. Strategy is a must.

SECRET #19 to Creative Leadership:
Going from a transactional contributor to being a leader who is strategic is one of the toughest things for most people to do. It forces you to go from a tactical, feet-on-the-floor approach to a more strategic, 30,000 foot perspective with an eye on the big picture—and obviously the skill set is different. Creative leaders understand that strategy is a teachable skill, and they take time to study it. They also know strategy is a creative process involving nearly limitless ideas. When combining creativity with teachability, the results can be mind-blowing. General Schwarzkopf was well known for his logical mind, but make no mistake about it, the man was wildly creative—and he surrounded himself with similarly minded people. Wildly creative people can sometimes be viewed as crazy as they explore the possibilities that other people ignore. Creative leaders recognize that they sometimes have to <u>sell</u> people on their unusual approaches, and they know resistance will be encountered. They stay patient.

SECRET #20

HUMOR

hu·mor (hyū'-mur)

1. something seen as funny or amusing.

HUMOR

Years ago, a friend approached me and told me she felt I had an unexplored gift for painting, so she took me to a craft store, bought a large canvas, and set me up in an open space to "release me" to become the painter she envisioned I would become. Her first assignment for me was to paint a self-portrait. After an hour or so of mental preparation, I went for it. Within 30 minutes, I was on the floor laughing so hard I almost needed medical attention. The portrait I created was so cartoon-like and hideous, there was no chance anyone would ever guess it was of me—or even that of a human.

It was the best investment of time I've made in a long while. I could have wasted the experience by beating myself up over my apparent inabilities, but instead I chose to use the situation in a more positive way.

While I'm not yet convinced I have an inner painter trying to come out, I am sold on the fact that humor is an under-used gift which can help all of us become comfortable with taking risks.

SECRET #20 to Creative Leadership:
Creative leaders are always pushing against the boundaries of current thinking, and that offers them tons of opportunities to either become critical of themselves or to laugh. CLs will most often choose to laugh because they know they live out on the edge—the place most people don't dare to go to. If they take themselves too seriously, they will end up just like everyone—in the "safe" zone where mediocrity reigns. CLs know their use of humor in uncertain times can serve as a stress ball for the entire department. It can ease tension and demonstrate that everything is going to be just fine no matter what is taking place. CLs can find humor in almost anything, and they encourage others to do the same. A CL is aware that research shows a little play at work is an overall productivity booster. They promote play whenever appropriate.

SECRET #21

COMMUNICATION

com·mu·ni·cate \(kə-mū-nə-kāt)

1. to convey a message by voice, gesture or other means.
2. to successfully share a message so it is understood.

COMMUNICATION

I think we sometimes give ourselves too much credit for our communications—speaking as though it is a guarantee everyone will understand what we've just communicated. And, of course, that couldn't be further from the truth.

When we look at the definition, it becomes clear that communication involves a satisfactory exchange in which the message is <u>understood</u>, not <u>mis</u>understood. If we're honest with ourselves, we send the wrong messages a lot.

Sending the wrong message can have devastating effects. What if our computerized traffic light systems occasionally put a green light up when a red light was warranted? It is easy to visualize the colossal mess that would surely follow.

We send the wrong <u>signals</u> all the time, and sometimes even the right signal is interpreted to be the wrong signal. In either case, it creates a mess—and we are responsible.

SECRET #21 to Creative Leadership:
The most fertile ground for miscommunication is when you come across as <u>un</u>approachable. If people don't feel the freedom to ask you for clarification, they will act based on the best info they have, and it might not be the most accurate or perhaps even up-to-date.

A creative leader is an individual think-tank. She absolutely thrives on unconventional problem-solving, and she brings to the table a much-needed *box-breaking* approach. But as she smashes paradigms, she remembers to slow down to make sure she organizes her thoughts before she shares them. She knows how easy it is to be misunderstood, and she is careful as she formulates her messages. Also, to be sure the conveyed messages land properly, she asks the intended receivers to summarize the message back to her so she can verify that it was properly understood. She takes no chances.

SECRET #22

SOLUTIONS

solve   (sŏlv)

1. to work something out to a successful conclusion.

SOLUTIONS

When I was growing up, my dad had a phrase he used to share with me whenever I was facing a difficult task. He'd say: "Son, throw everything at it but the kitchen sink!" In my youthful wisdom, I would then consider my situation and wonder how <u>throwing</u> anything—especially a kitchen sink— would help at all. Clearly, my dad was not endorsing a destructive approach. He was simply saying tackle this thing with everything you have—there *is* a solution.

When I was serving in the United States Air Force as a mechanic on B-1B bombers, I watched as my co-workers seemed to act on my father's advice only to execute it badly. They would troubleshoot problems half-way, and then they would change out part after part in an expensive guessing game until they landed on the problem-ending culprit. They weren't good at finding appropriate solutions, and their approach was really expensive for taxpayers.

Every problem has a *good* solution. You just might have to look really hard to find it. Random efforts don't work.

SECRET #22 to Creative Leadership:
Creative leaders know there's a really good chance they aren't the one with the best solution to the work situation they're grappling with, so they tap into the brainpower of the talented men and women on their team. Creative leaders are very good at finding out where the answer is buried, and they dig until it is found. CLs also know that great solutions involve deep brainstorming. They know that real brainstorming involves a STORM. They are aware that it can sometimes feel dangerous, <u>and</u> it can get a little messy before it gets better. But the CL is unafraid and undeterred. They love generating a flood of ideas. They aren't comfortable until the wave of ideas is so large that old, safe thinking is drowned out. A CL won't just throw the "kitchen sink" at a problem. They will throw "the whole house too."

SECRET #23

CULTURE

cul·ture   (kull'-chur)

1. a system of beliefs or a way of behaving within a group.
2. a customary approach within the structure of a team, group, family, society, etc.

CULTURE

When you walk into any home or business, it takes almost no time whatsoever to get a sense for the culture there—or what I've come to refer to as "the smell of the place."

There is a really good video on YouTube of Prof. Sumantra Ghoshal introducing this concept at the World Economic Forum in 2010. Describing culture, he said some businesses give off a feeling of being in downtown Calcutta in the middle of summer, while others make you want to skip, or create, or conquer something. It's the *smell of the place*—and the smell of the place is on everything.

If your culture is one of structure, boundaries and safe decisions, everyone in that place will give off that "smell." If, however, you invite workers to enjoy their workplace, take risks, innovate, compete, and have fun, the "smell" will be very different, and it will draw people to it. Imagine the "smell" at Google, Facebook, Domino's, or Apple. How does it compare to Walmart, Sears, or McDonald's?

Culture is everywhere—some good, some not so good. What places draw you in? Can you explain why?

SECRET #23 to Creative Leadership:
Creative leaders know the importance of culture, and they are keenly aware of "the smell of the place." They know that if the overall corporate culture isn't good, they shouldn't "throw in the towel" because a creative leader can create a positive sub-culture within their realm of influence, making it desirable for people to work in that company anyway.

Creative leaders are also mindful of the every-increasing expectation by senior leaders for innovation in the workplace, and the CL knows an unhealthy culture will stifle innovative efforts. CLs study other successful cultures, and they farm for the best ideas to *borrow* as they continually work to build their culture.

SECRET #24

ATTITUDE

at·ti·tude (at'-tə-tood)

1. a predisposed way of thinking or feeling about people, places or things.

ATTITUDE

Attitudes are learned tendencies we all have to favorably or unfavorably evaluate people, places, objects, or situations. Two people can experience the very same thing and then form totally different attitudes about it.

For instance, one person can think the waiter was well-mannered and helpful, and the other person might feel he was worthless. How so? These are learned tendencies—informally taught to us by our family, friends, society, etc.—and what we learn isn't always healthy for us. Keep in mind though, if it was learned, it can be unlearned, or at least altered or replaced by a new experience.

Some people complain about their jobs while others are grateful to have one. Some people whine about the rain outside, but others rejoice that their lawn is being watered free of charge. Do you see the thorns on the roses, or do you choose to see the roses despite the thorns?

While our attitudes are learned tendencies, they are also a choice. We are the ones who ultimately get to decide how we think, feel and behave.

SECRET #24 to Creative Leadership:
One of the most corruptive forces working against any team's success is someone with a negative attitude. Since an attitude is learned, even your most positive people can be adversely impacted by a naysayer. Creative leaders are always on the lookout for this. They find and influence the naysayer before the naysayer adversely impacts others.

Zig Ziglar, a world renowned motivational guru, said "Your attitude, not your aptitude, determines your altitude." So, consider the *altitude* at which you are flying. What can you do to soar even higher? What can you do to rise above the negativity around you? Can you influence others to join you?

SECRET #25

ACCOUNTABILITY

ac·count·able   (ǝc-cown'-tǝ-bull)

1. responsible to explain your actions or justify your behaviors.

ACCOUNTABILITY

As the policeman emotionlessly issued the speeding ticket to me, I remember getting really angry. So what if I was doing 82 mph in a 70 mph zone? Didn't he see the reckless rule-breakers flying by me as though I was practically standing still? Doesn't he have real criminals to catch? And what idiot decided 70 mph was the appropriate speed for this road? This is CRAZY!

Yes, crazy is a good word. It's crazy to imagine a person thinking someone else is to blame when it is clear he is the one who messed up and broke the rules. Crazier still is the fact that he is in good company because practically everyone does the same thing.

Ever blame the toaster for burning your toast when you are the one who turns the knobs and sets the levers, knowing a toasters function is to literally burn bread? Ever blame the traffic for causing you to be late when you know the traffic is horrible on that road every day, and you should leave earlier?

History holds that other people must force us into accountability because we don't willingly do so ourselves. Well, it is about time we reverse this trend and start becoming people who practice the art of self-accountability.

SECRET #25 to Creative Leadership:
You will see real progress in your workplace when you stop holding other people's feet to the fire and instead create a culture of self-accountability where every employee has a true awareness of his/her actions and is willing to accept responsibility for the things he or she does—good or bad.
Creative leaders know that self-accountability starts with a person being able to SEE what they need to change, and it then requires that person to take OWNership of that thing.

SECRET #26

SERVANTS

ser·vant \ˈsər-vənt\

1. a person in the service of another.

SERVANT

"Get me a goblet of something cool and refreshing, and roast a pig in my honor immediately!" said the man as he placed his order at the steakhouse.

Well, maybe he didn't say it that way, but that's how it sounds to me when people order their food in restaurants and act as though their money allows them to treat the person serving them like a peasant in the hire of King Henry VIII. Servers may not like serving rude people, but I'm amazed at how they almost always do so with a level of unrelenting kindness and grace. They seem to do so with a true *servant's* heart.

Comedian Tim Hawkins does a hilarious bit about people who get labeled as having a servant's heart. "They're the ones over there stackin' chairs after church on Sunday while everyone else watches," says Hawkins. He goes on to talk about how people want to avoid being labeled as having a servant's heart. The thing is, we should all be in the service of one another, and until we collectively decide it is a strength—not a weakness—to choose serving over being served, we will never quite reach our full potential.

SECRET #26 to Creative Leadership:
Creative leaders are intentionally focused on equipping, enabling and serving others. They give their time, talents, and their treasures, and they expect nothing in return. CLs know that the path to their own personal success is paved by the investment they make in others. Conversely, many   people in this world have a hoarder mentality. They live as though they must gather all that they can in life as their source of supply may somehow run out. Creative leaders, however, trust in an endless supply, so they don't worry about storing up anything. They simply give and they serve. They know their supply will never dry up, run out, shift, or minimize.

SECRET #27

DISCIPLINE

dis·ci·pline \'di-sə-plən\

1. a way of behaving that shows a willingness to obey rules or orders.
2. training that corrects, molds, or perfects the mental faculties or moral character.
3. orderly or prescribed conduct or pattern of behavior.

DISCIPLINE

Have you ever ironed your underwear into a four-inch block of perfection? I have. It was simultaneously the most useless and useful task I think I have ever done in my life. It was a daily ritual required of me when I first joined the United States Air Force.

The point of pressing your skivvies wasn't so you would have a wrinkle-free Hanes experience. We did this only so we could learn how to follow orders—something with which most 18-year old men struggle. In fact, pretty much everything we did was about instilling discipline in us.

The early days of my military career were marked with the fingerprints of imposed discipline. I did things because someone was watching, and there was a consequence for screwing up. Interestingly, at some point I began to do things because of a devotion to moral character and good form, not because someone was watching. Through this journey, the military taught me self-discipline. I now consciously hold myself accountable to do the right things.

SECRET #27 to Creative Leadership:
Many leaders spend a lot of time watching over others because those people still need imposed discipline. It's both exhausting and annoying to have to monitor people when they should be monitoring themselves. Perhaps it's time to pull out the *underwear* and have them start ironing—so to speak. CLs will assign them simple tasks with rigid requirements and less than pleasant outcomes if the tasks are not completed properly and within the time constraints outlined. It won't take long before self-discipline is formed since it always starts with the small things. But let's be honest, even creative leaders sometimes find themselves struggling to maintain their own level of discipline because they really enjoy getting lost imagining and creating. But a creative leader is quick to recognize the shift…and adjust.

SECRET #28

COURAGE

cour·age \'kər-ij, 'kə-rij\

1. mental or moral strength to venture, persevere, and withstand danger, fear, or difficulty.

COURAGE

The cowardly lion in the classic movie *The Wizard of Oz* is a great example of someone who is deeply afraid of practically everything, and his story most likely mirrors most people in one way or another. You see, we are all a little cowardly in some areas of our lives, and just like the fearful feline in the epic film, we don't typically realize that the courage we need is always right there inside of us.

Michael Wright, Head of Programming for TNT, TBS and Turner Classic Movies, is a great example of courage in the workplace. During one particular coaching session he had with me, Wright told me there are times when he knows the next thing out of his mouth is not going to be received well by his boss, but he says it anyway because his personal convictions won't let him withhold. He may not always be right, but his voice is always heard—and it's that kind of boldness that has fueled his meteoric rise in the industry.

Courage is hard to muster because it smacks in the face of uncertainty. After all, if we knew how things would be received, we wouldn't really need courage, now would we?

SECRET #28 to Creative Leadership:
If you examine your track record, do you see evidence that indicates you operate from a position of safety and self-preservation, or does the record show you courageously lead your team to accomplish the unimaginable? It takes courage to come up with ground-breaking, out-of-the-box solutions at which others might be inclined to laugh. Creative leaders press forward anyway. They know the courage they possess is the genesis of the value they bring. They aren't crazy, but they do take risks. Some CLs even live on the very edge of uncertainty where failure is just as close as success. But they weigh the rewards against the costs, and they take calculated leaps of faith. CLs foster this courageous mindset in others.

SECRET #29

ENTHUSIASM

en·thu·si·asm \in-ˈthü-zē-ˌa-zəm\

1. strong excitement about something; a strong feeling of active interest in something that you like or enjoy

ENTHUSIASM

Green Bay quarterback Brett Favre made history over and over again by smashing one record after another on his way to iconic status. As great as he was as the gun-slinging, risk-taker, what sports fans really loved about him was his unbridled enthusiasm for the game.

Watching Favre was like watching a 10-year old kid. Even after 20 years in the NFL, he jumped up and down after exciting plays that others on his team seemed to shrug off as just part of the job. One such display of enthusiasm came after Favre threw a touchdown pass and jubilantly ran by referee Pete Morelli giving him a low-five hand-slap. "I was just looking for someone to celebrate with," Favre said at the time. "He just happened to have stripes on." Perhaps Favre didn't realize you shouldn't get that excited in the NFL.

Near the end of his career, other players would sit in the locker room before the initial kickoff pondering Favre's encouraging, pre-game words. "Let's go have some fun," he would tell them. They apparently forgot it was a game, and they were supposed to have fun.

SECRET #29 to Creative Leadership:

Creative leaders get super excited when their team members hit a target, crush a competitor, land a big contract, or do pretty much anything worthy of a high-five. CLs know that if they want their employees to be excited, they must demonstrate excitement too. They make a big deal about behaviors they want to see repeated. If someone shows exceptional teamwork, the CL recognizes and rewards it. If a struggling performer finally finds that "next gear" and begins to deliver the required results, the CL sees it as a big deal, and he makes sure the achievement is given the proper attention. CLs are generally happy people who want to win and who look for things to celebrate.

SECRET #30

INTUITION

in·tu·i·tive \in-ˈtü-ə-tiv, -ˈtyü-\
1. an understanding without evidence.

INTUITION

How did mom always know?

Seriously, I really want an answer. The woman was like some sort of Golden Child with mystical powers to reveal everything I ever did. Like most kids, I always got caught.

We've all heard about women's intuition, right? Do they have some special sixth sense about them, or is their seemingly freakish ability grounded in something else? Hint: The answer lies somewhere in the middle.

First of all, there is absolute proof many people—not just women—have dreams or visions of futuristic events that ultimately do happen. I firmly believe this is a download from God—but since this isn't a book about spirituality, I will leave you to work that out for yourself.

Secondly, all other intuition falls into a big bucket called a *gut feeling*, and these "hunches" are based largely on your experience and knowledge. While it's true intuition is defined as understanding without evidence, our experience with something can give us a gut feeling even though we lack the evidence to support it. Most CEOs use this type of intuition to run their companies. In doing so, they are often right on the money—but sometimes their "hunch" is wrong.

SECRET #30 to Creative Leadership:
Creative leaders know they won't always have every piece of information they need. They trust their gut. If everything inside them says "go for it", they jump. When a creative leader holds back and doesn't trust their intuition, they often regret it—and it's in those times that they end up watching someone else running with the very idea they once had, and they are stuck watching their great results from the veritable sidelines. CLs aren't comfortable losing, so they trust what they know and what they *feel*.

SECRET #31

PATIENCE

pa·tience \ˈpā-shən(t)s\

1. the quality of being patient, as the bearing of provocation, annoyance, misfortune, or pain, without complaint, loss of temper, irritation, or the like.
2. quiet, steady perseverance; even-tempered care; diligence.

PATIENCE

I stopped by the grocery store the other day, picked up a few lunch items, and headed to the express lane to checkout. I was completely oblivious to the fact that the woman currently checking out in front of me had 40 or 50 items—I simply didn't care. As my indifference about the situation led my mind to wander toward other things, I suddenly heard the clerk begin to chastise the woman for exceeding the 15-item maximum for the express lane. Completely unaware she had stepped into the "fast lane", the woman began to apologize to me over and over as though she committed some sort of crime. "I'm so sorry," she said—at least ten times.

As I pondered this situation, I kept thinking to myself, "If people can't spare two extra minutes of their day for something as innocent as this without melting down, perhaps they're booking themselves a little too tightly.

Comedian Brian Regan has a great YouTube video in which he pokes fun at people who are so impatient they want to zap-fry their Pop Tarts in the microwave. "How long does it take to <u>toast</u> a Pop Tart?" Regan asks. "A minute? Can't wait that long?" Your schedule is definitely booked too tight.

SECRET #31 to Creative Leadership:
Creative leaders are known to be patient people, and that is likely attributable to all of the time they spend in the unknown where problems aren't solved in an instant, and great answers don't just fall from the sky. The creative leader knows that the things worth having in this life are worth waiting for—so they are patient. The CL is also careful to promote an atmosphere of patient expectation among all of her team members. She draws a hard line on the difference between being patient and being lazy. She insists on perseverance. The CL knows she must also fight people's desire for instant results with a mentality of delayed gratification.

SECRET #32

LANGUAGE

lan·guage \\'laŋ-gwij, -wij\\

1. any one of the systems of human language that are used and understood by a particular group of people.
2. the system of words or signs that people use to express thoughts and feelings to each other.
3. the words, their pronunciation, and the methods of combining them used and understood by a community.

LANGUAGE

While traveling through Baton Rouge, LA on my way to Shreveport, I did the unthinkable for a man—I stopped to ask for directions. I had taken some back roads and was so lost I had little hope of finding anything even resembling Shreveport. Swallowing my pride, I pulled over into a little gas station and went inside to get some help. After I spent a few seconds communicating my situation to the attendant, I listened carefully as he very kindly gave me what sounded like some detailed directions. I say "sounded like" because his accent was so heavy, I bet I didn't clearly understand one word of his nearly 90-second reply. I left belly-laughing.

The Bible teaches us about the power of language with the example of the Tower of Babel. Initially, the people were communicating so well, the tower they were building proved nothing would be impossible for them. So the Lord confused their language, and their progress came to a halt. In some ways, it's still like that today. But remember, you have the ability to do almost *anything* when your language isn't confused, and you can lead a team to produce awesomeness.

SECRET #32 to Creative Leadership:
Creativity has a language of its own, and it is rarely fully understood or appreciated at initial glance. The best part about it is that one creative *piece* can speak different things to different people but still not cause any confusion. Creative leaders are free-thinkers, and they inspire that in others. They know there isn't one right way to almost anything, so they don't get hung up looking for just one thing. CLs let people uniquely express themselves, and they listen carefully to everything that is said. They go on a mental journey with each person as they share, and you should too. Take time to be less impressed by what you think you have figured out and become more impressed by the thinking and the language of those around you. The possibilities are endless.

SECRET #33

VALUE

val·ue \ˈval-(ˌ)yü\

1. the relation of one part in a picture to another with respect to lightness and darkness.
2. something desirable.

VALUE

In 1929, the electronics company Zenith announced its new slogan: "The quality goes in before the name goes on." My question to you is: "Does it"? Is a Zenith television set automatically a quality product because Zenith says they put the quality in it? I mean who gets to decide what is quality and what is junk? Does Zenith get to do that for us, or is it something consumers must decide for themselves? Clearly, it's our decision. We assess it, and then decide to approve or disapprove of both the product and its price. We do this with everything—physical products, relationships, the weather, etc. We assess the *value* of all things, and that assessment can change based on our present circumstances. Value is not inherent in anything.

To a wealthy person, $5 is completely unimportant, but to a homeless person, it might represent a week's worth of food. To a person living in Florida, a palm tree is just another tree, but to people living in the Midwest, a palm tree is the symbol of relaxation and peace. The beauty—or should I say *value*— is in the eye of the beholder. With value, there is no right and wrong.

SECRET #33 to Creative Leadership:
Creative leaders are keenly aware of the incredible diversity in people's thinking, and they know it takes a lot of effort and a whole lot of creativity to get everyone on the same page during a project. While it's true that people can widely differ on almost everything, there is typically a middle ground to be explored. Consider religion for example. People have intense emotions about which faith is the right one, but almost everyone can agree that love and kindness are bedrock principles. Politics is largely the same. Some people are way on the left; some are way on the right—some are in the middle, but all agree that freedom is paramount. They just don't always agree on how to get there. Find the middle.

SECRET #34

LINES

Line \\ˈlīn\\

1. a long narrow mark on a surface.
2. the course or direction of something in motion.
3. a state of agreement or conformity.
4. a boundary of an area.

LINE

People seriously underestimate the power of a line. After all, it's just a mark spanning a distance and taking any form whatsoever along the way, right? Wrong.

Actually, lines are so very much more. They are defining, dividing, and expressive. They even tell stories. There is a wonderful poem by Linda Ellis called *Making the Most of Your Dash* in which she makes reference to the little line on a tombstone between a person's date of birth and their date of death—the "dash." Think about the power of that line and what it represents. A life filled with success and with failure, happiness and heartbreak, good decisions and ones of regret.

We can choose to let lines separate us too—such as state lines, battle lines, or the hard lines of our attitudes. Or we can use lines to draw our eyes to the beauty of architecture, landscapes, the written word, illustrations or any other place where conformity yields to freedom.

SECRET #34 to Creative Leadership:
Creative leaders are careful NOT to draw "lines in the sand" for their employees. They are mindful not to set parameters which overly dictate direction, contain creativity, or rush outcomes. Creative leaders are even cautious sometimes of setting <u>minimum</u> expectations for team members because, for some, it can become the target to achieve rather than a barrier over which to leap on the way to much higher results. CLs know those *lines* are actually chains which can unintentionally stifle creativity and an employee's ability to freely explore. Author G. K. Chesterton once wrote: "Art, like morality, consists in drawing the line somewhere." Hey, your lines might be letters in a journal, sketches in a notebook, paint on a canvas, chalk on a blackboard, etc. But make no mistake, you <u>must</u> draw the line—somewhere.

SECRET #35

HARMONY

har·mo·ny \ˈhär-mə-nē\

1. a pleasing combination or arrangement of different things.

HARMONY

13 years.

That's how long you can expect to wait for tickets to see the highly acclaimed Vienna Philharmonic perform its stunning repertoire of jaw-dropping musical compositions with absolute symphonic perfection.

The group is comprised of approximately 100 musicians—each possessing such expert ability, they could no doubt make a handsome living on their individual effort alone. And yet, they choose to invest their talent in a collective sound where their contribution is essentially unidentifiable on its own.

These masters yearn for the unmistakable harmony which cannot be achieved by their instrument alone. Instead, they lend their individual sounds to the group, and the conductor weaves them all together.

SECRET #35 to Creative Leadership:
In business, you see a lot of experts doing their own thing, achieving individual successes without really considering the potential synergy of a collective approach. I'd encourage you to have your team watch a few minutes of the Vienna Philharmonic and then discuss how they might model what they've seen. YouTube has some great videos of them.

Creative leaders know that harmony does not involve the surrendering of unique talents or contributions simply so that someone gets to have things done their way. Conversely, CLs know that harmony means lending your gifts to the greater effort. CLs never ask anyone to lose themselves as they contribute to the team efforts. In fact, a CL will find ways for their employees to go solo whenever their unique gifts are best released through individual efforts. After all, even the Vienna Philharmonic has segments with solos.

SECRET #36

DRIVE

drive \ˈdrīv\

1. to carry on or through energetically.
2. to repulse, remove, or cause to go by force, authority, or influence.
3. to exert inescapable or coercive pressure on.
4. to give shape or impulse to.

DRIVE

In just seven short years, Dan Pink, the provocative New York Times bestselling author, has turned our thinking upside down when it comes to the topic of drive—a.k.a. motivation.

In his book, *Drive*, Pink says "...carrots and sticks are so last century." This reference to the behavior modification methods used to get horses to follow commands has long been an approach business leaders have also taken with employees. You wouldn't, of course, use a carrot or a stick, but the premise was that every person is moved by something, so find out what moves them.

Pink, on the other hand, offers a new way of thinking about developing a person's drive. He says drive is comprised of three key elements:

Autonomy: Freedom to direct your own outcome.

Mastery: The urge to get better at something that matters.

Purpose: The yearning to do what we do in the service of something larger than ourselves.

SECRET #36 to Creative Leadership:

It might be time to put down your *carrots* and start approaching employee drive differently. One thing is for sure: You will need to really know your people in order to employ Pink's approach effectively. A good starting point would be to read his book. Creative leaders study motivation, and they are keenly in tune with their employees. Like most leaders, a CL can see enthusiasm or apathy, but the difference is that CLs always take action based on what they see, hear, and feel. They don't hesitate to ask questions in an effort to understand their employees. It shows they care. It also gives the CL insight into the person and their desire for Autonomy, Mastery, and Purpose. A creative leader finds out what lights a person's fire, and then they make sure they do everything in their power to keep that fire burning.

SECRET #37

RESOURCEFULNESS

re·source·ful \ri-ˈsȯrs-fəl, -ˈzȯrs-\

1. able to deal well with new or difficult situations and to find solutions to problems.
2. capable of devising ways and means.

RESOURCEFULNESS

Secret agent Angus MacGyver—played by actor Richard Dean Anderson in the 1980's television series by the same name—was perhaps the most resourceful person you'll ever come across, real or fictional. Why? Well, MacGyver is someone who could fix anything—a toaster, a jet engine, or a "ticking" nuclear weapon on its way to detonation. The best part about watching the educated scientist was not the fact that he *could* fix those things but rather *how* he did it. Amazingly, the solutions almost always had something to do with duct tape and a Swiss Army pocket knife.

While his accomplishments were often fictitious and, at times, hard to believe, MacGyver does provide us with some important lessons by which to live.

First, whenever you are facing circumstances which seem impossible, don't give up—MacGyver always pressed on to find a solution. You can too.

Second, always be prepared. Mac was never without his "go to" tools. He was so well known for having the duct tape and SA knife that anyone who fixes something with them these days is still likely to be called MacGyver.

Third, think unconventionally. MacGyver's solutions were always mind blowing. He may have used the same tools a lot, but the way he used them varied with each situation.

SECRET #37 to Creative Leadership:
Creative leaders make sure they give their employees ample opportunity to demonstrate their ingenuity—and then they stand back and watch! When the pressure is off, and the ideas are flowing, amazing things are in store for sure. There is no doubt MacGyver was wildly creative and produced amazing results, but perhaps he leaned too heavily on just two of his favorite tools. Do you rely too much on any one way to solve your problems? Creative leaders utilize all of their tools.

SECRET #38

SHAPE

shape \ˈshāp\

1. to give a particular form; to work with (a material) in order to make something from it.
2. to make (something, such as a plan) by a process of careful thought.

SHAPE

About 15 years ago, on a whim I joined a friend who wanted to go to an intro class for wood carving. Being a manly man, all I needed to hear were the words "wood" and "knives", and I was sold. As I settled into my seat around the table, I was not at all prepared for the life lesson I would learn from the seemingly innocuous contact between blade and pine.

After running us through all of the typical safety tips, the instructor spoke to us about shape. "The object you see in your mind" he said confidently, "is already in that block of wood. All you need to do is chip away until it is revealed. It will take shape." A few minutes later I would learn that the process of wood carving is actually called *revealing*.

As I sat there peacefully whittling away at my block, I couldn't help but think about how people are the same way. There is so much potential beneath the surface—we just need to take shape. And just when we think our *shape* has been fully realized, a little more "carving" reveals a refined—or even a completely different—shape. We're all a work in progress.

SECRET #38 to Creative Leadership:
It might be easy to look at the people around you and judge them for what you can see today, but creative leaders refuse to look solely at surface-level things. Instead, they routinely give thought to what it is they don't yet see. They study the potential in people and things. They consider what a person could become if only someone would invest some effort in helping that person grow—maybe through a bit of *whittling*. CLs also imagine projects and their possible outcomes even if the current state is bleak. They are not deterred by anything that is in mid-state, meaning it has not yet reached its full potential. A CL is never fully satisfied until all of the *carving* is complete, and the work is fully finished. Then she smiles.

SECRET #39

TEXTURE

tex·ture \'teks-chər\

1. the visual or tactile surface characteristics and appearance of something.
2. the way something feels when you touch it.
3. the various parts of a song, poem, movie, etc., and the way they fit together.

TEXTURE

You may not realize it, but people are obsessed with texture. So much so, the word is now being overused to describe non-physical things by physical terms.

For instance, we speak of relationships and appearance in terms of temperature: "She is so <u>hot</u>. He is as <u>cold</u> as ice. I've <u>warmed</u> up to that company."

We even take it further into character traits with phrases like: "He has a <u>rough</u> exterior," and "That competitor has gone <u>soft</u>." Think of the American classic film *True Grit*, starring actor John Wayne. *Grit* was the word used to describe the courage and resolve of the character Wayne played in the movie. Grit, by the way, is the term we also use to classify sandpaper—an item with all kinds of texture.

We love texture so much that we have a desire to touch everything we see—it helps us *connect* with the item. I remember visiting Blarney Castle in Ireland where I, like millions of others, couldn't resist hovering precariously upside down to kiss the stone which was fabled to give people the gift of gab. The once rough stone had been kissed so many times by soft lips, it had become unbelievably smooth. Our love for texture can even change the texture.

SECRET #39 to Creative Leadership:
Did you know that every person, every team, and every company has a *texture* to it? Your texture is the feeling people have when they have an encounter with you. How might people describe your texture? And how does your personal *texture* interact with the texture of those around you? Can you mix the textures without losing the individual value of each? What happens when you do so? Creative leaders are ever mindful of the way people interact, and they are careful to ensure no one's *texture* wears on anyone else in a way that causes unwelcome friction. Unwelcome wear is very different from wear which produces a shine.

SECRET #40

VULNERABILITY

vul·ner·a·ble \ˈvəl-n(ə-)rə-bəl, ˈvəl-nər-bəl\

1. capable of being hurt.
2. open to attack or damage.

VULNERABILITY

Vulnerability just might be the toughest of all of these 100 words. For some of us, it can even be painful to say the word.

Brené Brown, author of the book *Daring Greatly,* was featured on a Ted Talk video for her research on the topic of vulnerability. In the video, Brown asserts that vulnerability is the core of shame, fear and our struggle for worthiness but adds that surprisingly it also appears that vulnerability is the birthplace of joy, of creativity, of belonging, and of love. She says that those who choose to make themselves vulnerable always have a strong sense of worth first. Vulnerability never precedes worthiness.

Brown's research also suggests vulnerable people have the courage to be imperfect, they have compassion for themselves first before demonstrating it for others, and they feel connection as a result of their own authenticity.

One other important point she makes is that those who choose to numb themselves to vulnerability through spending, eating or self-medicating simultaneously numb themselves to joy, gratitude and happiness. The numbing process affects all areas; you can't pick and choose—it's not something you can selectively control.

SECRET #40 to Creative Leadership:
The leadership ladder emotionlessly insists you put yourself out there for public scrutiny and critique. But don't fool yourself; thick skin has nothing to do with it—you must feel worthy or fear will grip you. You must be aware that your outward ability to handle the heavy criticism you receive is not necessarily a good barometer of what's going on inside you. You must do a gut check of your self-worth, or at some point, you will derail. Creative leaders are authentic, and they are perfectly imperfect. They become vulnerable because they know it is the very thing which makes them joyful and wildly creative. EVERYONE can be a creative leader.

SECRET #41

DESIGN

de·sign \di-ˈzīn\

1. to devise for a specific function or end.
2. to create, fashion, execute, or construct according to plan.
3. to conceive and plan out in the mind.

DESIGN

I believe we are all created with a unique design—devised to fulfill a God-given plan. Even if you don't believe in God, you can't deny the fact each person you meet is different from every other. Some people are magnets who draw us to them, while others have a bit of a repelling factor. In either case, our personal design impacts the human experience, and creating great human experiences is a big issue these days— every business grapples with it.

For example, Kaiser Permanente, the largest health maintenance organization in the U.S., hired IDEO, a Palo Alto, CA design firm to help them with "their patient experience." KP had designed great buildings all over the country, but they had completely failed to create a design centered on the very people for whom they exist. As a result, half naked people were sitting in cold rooms for up to 30 minutes needlessly contemplating the painful procedures that might await them. IDEO partnered with KP and had doctors and nurses experience this treatment as actual patients. It didn't take long for them to see what to change.

SECRET #41 to Creative Leadership:
It's really easy for us to jump into execution mode before we have a fully-baked design or plan. After all, we want to be seen as productive. Take it from me, slow down and proceed very deliberately because design really matters.

People sometimes tear up their designs and start over if they become frustrated with the way things are coming together. It totally slows them down. Creative leaders avoid these forced restarts—they simply morph the design they already have in hand. They modify it to become what it should be rather than abandon it altogether. They design and redesign until they construct a work of art. That approach takes a lot of patience, but it propels things forward much faster.

83

SECRET #42

COLOR

col·or \ˈkə-lər\

1. a phenomenon of light or visual perception that enables one to differentiate otherwise identical objects.
2. an appearance of authenticity.
3. the aspect of the appearance of objects and light sources that may be described in terms of hue, lightness, and saturation for objects and hue, brightness, and saturation for light sources.

COLOR

Do we all see things the same way? Is the color red the exact same red everyone sees, or is red actually blue to someone else who is simply calling it red because that's all he or she knows? It's a deep question.

Science has proven we all differentiate color by the use of things called *rods* and *cones* in our eyes. It has also been proven that the number of rods and cones varies greatly from person to person increasing the chances for us to see the same thing differently. But, the good news is that the brain takes over to compensate, and like a super-computer begins to work out patterns to fill in the information our eyes fail to provide. And, it does a great job at it.

It's hard to know for sure if we all see red in the exact same shade and saturation, but we do know most people have strong reactions to the use of colors. After all, the use of color is a major consideration in almost any industry.

SECRET #42 to Creative Leadership:
In art, the opacity of a color is a reference to the amount of light allowed through the color or image. If it is opaque, it is essentially impenetrable. If, however, it is translucent, it becomes semi-transparent—somewhat see-through. A creative leader seeks to model the latter as much as possible. They strive for transparency as it builds trust while an opaque-like style can build walls.

If your workplace could be identified by a color, what would it be? What neurological pattern-making might be at work to help you come to that conclusion? How could you change the *color* if you don't like it? These might seem like bizarre questions, but creative leaders think in uncommon ways. They study things other leaders are indifferent toward, and they make connections to things which seem totally disconnected. CLs look for sources of light and inspiration. They find *color* even in black and white circumstances.

SECRET #43

RHYTHM

rhythm   \'ri-thəm\

1. a regular, repeated pattern of events, changes, activities, etc.
2. movement, fluctuation, or variation marked by the regular recurrence or natural flow of related elements

RHYTHM

Even from the time we're born, we all seem to love rhythm. Babies love to lay on their mother's chest and listen to her heartbeat; little children rock back and forth in stationary chairs; adults constantly tap their hands and feet to the beat of music. Rhythm is powerful.

I distinctly remember marching in Basic Military Training and listening to the sound of hundreds of boot heels striking the ground at the same precise moment. I also remember the drill sergeant telling us to get out of rhythm and simply walk as we crossed over a bridge on the base. You see, physics has shown that rhythmic marching—hundreds of simultaneous heel strikes—is so powerful it can create an oscillation of sine waves strong enough to collapse a bridge.

The power of rhythm is drastically underestimated. Think about your favorite music group. Who is the star? The lead singer, right? Yet every leader singer will tell you it is the drummer who is the director for every song. The singers can't just go off and do their own thing. Like everyone else in the band, they listen carefully to the rhythm created by the percussionist. The beat knits them all together in seamless fashion. Without rhythm, they would be a chaotic mess.

SECRET #43 to Creative Leadership:
Creative leaders set and maintain the rhythm of their workplaces. They know that if they have lousy *timing*, everyone around them will probably be out of sync too. Employees yearn for a natural, predictable pattern in their leaders, and CLs are careful to provide it. Having said that, it should come as no small surprise that creative leaders sometimes march to the beat of their own drummer as they let their   imaginations run wild. Hey, the workplace needs a leader who does that. CLs just can't forget to circle back and join the group effort too.

SECRET #44

BALANCE

bal·ance \ˈba-lən(t)s\

1. a state in which different things occur in equal or proper amounts or have an equal or proper amount of importance; an aesthetically pleasing integration of elements.
2. the ability to move or to remain in a position without losing control or falling.

BALANCE

At the 1996 Olympic Games in Atlanta, Georgia, U.S. gymnast, Shannon Miller, did something the world thought was impossible. She became the first American ever to win a gold medal on the balance beam as she defeated the seemingly unbeatable competition from Romania.

As I watched her victory unfold, I wondered how anyone could balance on a 4" wide beam high off the ground while doing mind-blowing, hands-free flips, twists and turns. *I can barely balance my checkbook or eat a balanced diet*, I remembered thinking. I was incredibly impressed with the discipline she had for her craft.

But then my thoughts quickly shifted to how out of balance her life must have been for her to get that good. Surely, she sacrificed much of her time with friends and family in her pursuit. It's odd how unbalanced we all can be—even someone with the rare balancing abilities of a Shannon Miller. It takes effort to keep from *leaning* too far left or right in any particular area of our lives.

SECRET #44 to Creative Leadership:
When my uber creative friends get into a flow, they often lose a sense of balance in their lives while they hyper-focus on their creations. Showers, food, friends, and family all take a back seat in those moments. This approach may allow a laser-like focus, but it can be unhealthy—for many reasons.

Creative leaders, however, strive for self-awareness to maintain their balance. They know they are wired to burn the candle at both ends as they tackle important projects, solve pesky problems, or overcome personal challenges. CLs know their personal tendency to isolate from others in these moments, but they don't. Instead, they invite others to work with them. They know their candle loses nothing when it lights another one. So, they offer their <u>light</u>, and they get more <u>light</u> in return.

SECRET #45

CONSISTENCY

con·sis·ten·cy \kən-ˈsis-tən(t)-sē\

1. agreement or harmony of parts or features to one another or a whole.
2. ability to be asserted together without contradiction.

CONSISTENCY

Tiger Woods. It's difficult to find someone who doesn't know Tiger. His fame is attributed to one thing—consistency...well, and _in_consistency.

Until Tiger joined the tour, any player might win on any given week. Once Woods' game got dialed in though, he was so consistently good, he was nearly impossible to beat. He was such a threat every week that players leading by as many as eight strokes going into the final round would completely fall apart with the _Tiger_ chasing them. True to his name, he would _devour_ them. Woods was so good, if he didn't win, his second or third place finish would be the topic of all of the water-cooler conversations the next day, not the winner.

His game—and his life, it seemed—was in complete harmony. Then, after a shocking revelation about in-consistency in his personal life, the consistency of his golf game suddenly disappeared too. I'm not here to bash Woods. I love him as a golfer, and I believe we all mess up in life, and we deserve second chances. My point here is that consistency is tough to maintain because it often requires intense focus. When Tiger lost his focus, he lost his edge—he lost nearly all of his consistency, and winning went with it.

SECRET #45 to Creative Leadership:
One thing is for sure, people like predictability—they like consistency in their leaders. When they aren't sure what to expect from you each day, YOU just might be the topic of unproductive water-cooler conversation. Creative leaders get results because they dive into the things others choose to sidestep, and their approaches are often unpredictable because what they are working on is filled with uncertainty, and it needs to be met with an unconventional approach. A CL knows most people are uncomfortable working in ways that aren't familiar. CLs stretch people just enough for them to grow without causing them to snap.

SECRET #46

BRAINSTORMING

brain·storm \-,st□rm\

1. an idea that someone thinks of suddenly.
2. a temporary state of confusion; a period of unclear thinking.
3. a violent transient fit of insanity.

BRAINSTORMING

Like most people, I have participated in countless brainstorming sessions. For 25 years, I've joined my colleagues at numerous companies as we hunkered down and came up with what I believed were masterful ideas. Now, looking back, I can confidently tell you we were not really brainstorming at all. To be honest, by definition, our efforts could hardly be considered a brain-*mist*, much less a storm. Sadly, the same just might be true of you and your colleagues.

The first definition on the opposing page is where we typically stop when we think of brainstorming, and that's why the majority of our ideas seem so safe, so doable, and so much like what our competitors put together in their sessions too. But that's not where we should stop—those safe ideas are only the launching pad. We need to push to the edge of uncertainty.

"Storms" are created by a collision of high pressure and low pressure systems which can create powerful winds, electro-static discharges, uncertainty, and even panic. Storms take us out of our comfort zone and place us in a state of vulnerability, and it's in that state we see our true strength.

SECRET #46 to Creative Leadership:
Creative leaders know that for them to beat the competition, they can't always play it safe—they've got to get their team members to think about solutions that might appear impossible—maybe even *dangerous*. Think about it, nearly every great invention was once considered impossible. CLs look beyond the low hanging fruit which anyone can grab. They look at the fruit which is out of reach—maybe even the fruit that no one else can even see. A creative leader hates working with safe ideas. They view them as boring and uninspiring. CLs know you can't be innovative and cutting-edge by using old ways of thinking.

SECRET #47

ESSENTIALS

es·sen·tial \i-ˈsen(t)-shəl\

1. extremely important and necessary.
2. something necessary, indispensable, or unavoid-able.

ESSENTIALS

During one of our recent—and all too common—government shutdowns, we heard a lot about the staffing of *essential* personnel and the furlough of non-essentials. After just a little digging, I discovered that we have 2.7 million federal employees, 800k of which are not essential. That really got me thinking. If they aren't essential to us, why do we have them at all? While I'm not knocking those employees and their contributions, it does beg the question, doesn't it?

In the corporate world we see much of the same thing. We see overspending on non-essential things, and then when times get tight, big cuts come as companies get rid of their "fat". Let's face it, if a position can't be tied to the key results needed by the business, it really isn't necessary. Keep in mind that even positions like custodial services <u>are</u> connected to the bottom line—operating without them isn't possible. Trash would pile up, the restrooms would become shelters for disease, and morale would surely crash.

SECRET #47 to Creative Leadership:
Besides personnel, we also have essential and non-essential tasks. I would encourage you to take a good look around to see where you could be saving time and money. At some point, you will be called upon to account for all resources and how they are being used.

Creative leaders are like chefs in a world class kitchen. They know if they have too much or too little of anything in their recipe, their risk spoiling the whole dish. Like chefs, CLs *taste-test* constantly as they create, asking themselves if what they added—or didn't add—made the outcome better or worse. In your workplace, do you *taste* your creations, *consuming* them as your audience would?

SECRET #48

CONVERGENCE

con·ver·gent \-jənt\

1. tending to move toward one point or to approach each other

CONVERGENCE

Apple Inc. generates a lot of enthusiasm about every 6-12 months when they announce either a new device or an upgrade to an existing one. As a result, they create a feeding-frenzy atmosphere as tens of thousands of people wait in line to be the first to own the latest Apple product. People come from far away *converging* on stores around the globe.

While coming together to rally behind a product is all well and good, the word convergence is more typically used when describing team dynamics and collaboration. You might think of <u>this</u> convergence in the same way we merge vehicles in traffic.

For example, consider the vast network of roads and signs throughout a busy metropolitan area. We are all trying to go somewhere using them, but we won't be successful if we don't find a way to <u>merge</u> with each other and gradually weave together, accelerating at times and yielding at others.

In a team environment, if we all come to the table with wildly different ideas, we must find a way to merge our thoughts to produce the best possible outcome. We can't hold too tightly to our own ideas, or an *accident* might occur.

SECRET #48 to Creative Leadership:
Some people think *convergence* means surrendering their own identity for group-think—not true. A creative leader helps people understand the merit of all contributions and the value behind the best input, regardless of who provided it. Convergence is not a contest to win or lose. Instead, it is a mutual point toward which all parties head in an effort to come to a shared understanding—the common ground upon which to collaboratively build. Without convergence, people would force their opinions on others without regard for how it made them feel. If everyone didn't feel the need to move closer together in thought, divisiveness would rule the day, and teamwork would all but fade away. One word: Politics.

97

SECRET #49

OPENNESS

Open \\'ō-pən, -pᵊm\\

1. having no enclosing or confining barrier; accessible on all or nearly all sides
2. being in a position or adjustment to permit passage.
3. completely free from concealment; exposed to general view or knowledge.
4. exposed or vulnerable to attack or question.

OPENNESS

Ever hear the age-old speech from your boss about his open-door policy? Why is that speech needed? Any chance it is because he is selling something no one is buying? If he was an open person, everyone around him would feel free to reach out to him. When you think about it, having a policy on your openness is pretty much laughable.

Years ago, I caught myself in a routine of trying to convince people that I was an "open" person—I was effectively trying to sell people on the value of sharing their thoughts with an open, caring person like me. And then I realized something very important—I was not really *open* at all. In fact, if I was anything it was closed-minded.

It hit me like a ton of bricks. I discovered I didn't share much with others because I was not willing to make myself vulnerable to them, and I also had a host of other barriers I had *set up* which made approaching me a monumental task.

I came to the realization that open people don't need to tell other people they are an open person—their actions simply demonstrate it.

SECRET #49 to Creative Leadership:
Stop pretending you are an open person and just be one. The transparency you will create among your team members will be refreshing and productive.

Creative leaders put themselves "out there" for all to see, and their consistent vulnerability is the genesis of open dialogue between them and their employees. A creative leader listens well and has established a *safe place* for direct conversation. People share with people who are transparent about their own shortcomings, and who are slow to judge others. CLs are thoughtful, mature, measured, and, of course, accessible. Their <u>door</u> is always open, and they need not tell anyone about it. People just know.

SECRET #50

FLEXIBILITY

flex·i·ble \ˈflek-sə-bəl\

1. capable of bending or being bent
2. willing to change or to try different things
3. yielding to influence

FLEXIBILITY

A friend of mine does a lot of the custom woodworking on multi-million dollar homes in Colorado Springs, Colorado, and I had the chance to see him work his magic on one particular afternoon. As I observed, I saw him do something I thought was absolutely impossible—he bent hardwood. And he bent it a lot.

My previous experience with hardwood was that when you push or pull it past a certain point, it *announces* its stress by loudly cracking or splitting. Duane, on the other hand, was able to *influence* the wood to change its shape by heating, steaming, and clamping it into new form. Who knew? I thought wood was inflexible, but as it turns out, it <u>can</u> flex.

At times, we all have a certain amount of inflexibility about us, and we should stop to reflect why. We should ask ourselves if there is any sound rationale to the rigid positions we sometimes take, or—like a piece of hardwood—we could choose to bend a little and vulnerably expose ourselves to some potential *breakage*. Most likely, we won't break in the process, and we just mind find that we like the new *form* we have taken along the way.

SECRET #50 to Creative Leadership:
"My way or the highway" is a great line for a movie, but it is a sad one-liner if delivered by a leader in the workplace. Creative leaders know they weren't put in their leadership roles because they have all the right answers, so they don't present their thoughts and opinions as anything more than possible options. They don't *draw hard lines in the sand* on what they believe as they know the best answers are usually a hybrid formed from the collective contributions received from various different sources. While very flexible on most things, CLs are <u>not</u> flexible to a fault. They know they can't flex on some things like accountability, self-discipline, hard work, results, collaboration, respect, etc.

SECRET #51

AWARENESS

aware \ə-ˈwer\

1. knowing that something (such as a situation, condition, or problem) exists.
2. having or showing realization, perception, or knowledge

AWARENESS

I am not a big fan of horror films. Actually, I am not a fan of them at all—they totally creep me out. One particular movie that pushed me over the edge was the 1979 original version of *When a Stranger Calls*, starring actress Carol Kane. Hey, am I the only one on this planet who thinks it's not a good idea to "check the children" when a psychopathic caller dials you, the babysitter, and advises you to do so?

One thing is for sure: Almost every victim in every horror film I've seen has a deplorable lack of awareness. Seriously, how many times have you screamed at the screen in a theater trying to warn the future victims there is a killer standing right behind them? Despite your noble efforts, they just aren't <u>aware</u>—and, well, bad things happen.

Being *in the dark* isn't something reserved exclusively for horror films. We, too, sometimes operate in a state of *blindness* to the things going on around us, and the results can prove to be almost as devastating. It is critical for us to utilize all of our senses—even the sixth sense of intuition—to keep ourselves in the know as much as possible.

SECRET #51 to Creative Leadership:
Are your eyes and ears open and fine-tuned? Are you watching market trends and monitoring office gossip? Have you positioned yourself to be fully protected from all *threats* to your team's success? You must maintain constant awareness. Creative leaders can sometimes hyper-focus on tasks while they work with great speed, and that can have serious negative effects if they don't watch for the *storms* behind the rainbows they might be *painting*. A CL must move at a pace fast enough to produce great results but slow enough to allow him to assess, and react to, all of the things within his span of control. Forward progress is awesome, but CLs remember to look behind them for any *danger* closing in.

SECRET #52

COMPLIANCE

com·pli·ant \kuh m-plahy-uh nt\
1. complying; obeying, obliging, or yielding, especially in a submissive way.

COMPLIANCE

For most of my life, I never removed "The Tag". The tag I'm referring to is the one that annoyingly protrudes from most pillows, comforters, linens and mattresses. It's the quintessential warning label which threatens federal charges for removing it. What's crazy is that I was totally compliant about something that didn't even apply to me, the consumer. The warning on the tag was only for the seller to heed.

Yes, I agree it's crazy to have complied with something so silly for so long, but a quick internet search shows there are ridiculous numbers of people who've bowed to the same tag for years. Are you one? If so, why?

We all have an inner barometer for right and wrong, and since most of us seem to avoid behaviors with consequences, we naturally tend to be compliant. There are, of course, some areas in each of us where we raise the "I don't care" flag and just throw caution to the wind. Fortunately though, for most people, when the consequences of their actions will be harsh, they do find themselves doing what they are supposed to do.

SECRET #52 to Creative Leadership:

For anyone in leadership, you really need to know that forced compliance is not the way—it won't last much longer than the time it takes for you to leave the room. If your employees don't understand why they need to do something, make sure you take the time to explain it. If you don't, they might just give you a mediocre effort OR no effort at all. Creative leaders avoid focusing on compliance because they know it doesn't feel good to their employees. CLs know that if they want people to enjoy their work and contribute insane amounts of effort to it, then it must be fun and inspiring. A CL is careful about the people she surrounds herself with, so she isn't working with people who need monitoring. Instead, she hires passionate people who, if anything, need to be held back a bit from moving too quickly and missing key things.

SECRET #53

TEAM

Team \ˈtēm\

1. a group of people who work together.
2. a number of persons associated together in work or activity.
3. to yoke or join in a team; to put together in a coordinated ensemble.
4. marked by devotion to teamwork rather than individual achievement.

TEAM

There's no "I" in team. We've heard that cliché over and over again, right? So, why is it most businesses still seem to have a significant number of people in them who have their own agendas and work more for personal gain than for the good of the team? I think it's because people are afraid of missing an opportunity for their individual contributions to get noticed, and they feel that if they aren't noticed, they won't be promoted or otherwise rewarded. It's a fear of loss. So, in a self-promoting fashion, they work for personal gain. Hey, if you're working solo on a project, you can showcase yourself however you want, but when on a team, your efforts must blend with those of the people around you.

Think about the quarterback of a sports team. He may be the recognized superstar, but despite his expert skills, he can't hike, handoff, or pass the ball to himself—there are a collection of other players on the field whose contributions are really what make or break each and every play. If just one player misses a blocking assignment, a play which could have led to a score might result in a significant loss. Every player has a vital role, and no one succeeds alone on a team.

SECRET #53 to Creative Leadership:
Creative leaders take the time to recognize their star players, but they are careful about how they do it. Sometimes the praise is public, and sometimes it's private. CLs always take the time to recognize great individual contributions, but they are mindful about over-praising any single contributor in a public setting as it could create unintended resentment from other team members. CLs also look for the unsung heroes— team members who offer up great contributions but either due to circumstances or the quietness of their character, these folks have flown under the radar of recognition. The CL looks to make sure these contributions get the attention they deserve. CLs also find ways to recognize the WHOLE team.

SECRET #54

PATTERNS

pat·tern   \'pa-tərn\

1. the regular and repeated way in which something happens or is done.
2. a form or model proposed for imitation.
3. a discernible coherent system based on the intended interrelationship of component parts.

PATTERNS

I love airplanes—always have, always will. In 2003, I remember piloting a Piper Warrior single engine aircraft from a little runway in Schaumburg, Illinois—just a few miles from Chicago's busy O'Hare airport.

As I was in the traffic pattern on the downwind leg setting up for a landing, I briefly glanced down at my instrument panel to check my speed and upon looking up saw another light aircraft on a collision course with mine. After taking evasive maneuvers, my mind raced with thoughts of why the other pilot would be so off course—so "out of the pattern". While I survived that situation, it could have been horrific. Patterns seem to rule our lives—and a break in pattern can be very messy—maybe even catastrophic.

We're trained to look for patterns at a very early age. Even today's phone apps for kids have lessons on patterns. Shark, lamb, fish. Shark...lamb...? What's next in the pattern? Sound familiar?

We even train our brains for "breaks" in pattern. Do you remember the show Sesame Street and its familiar segment: "One of these things is not like the other..."? You see, we like looking for what is out of place.

SECRET #54 to Creative Leadership:
Everyone on your team has a predictable pattern of behavior. Have you taken time to notice it in each person? Doing so will greatly help you lead them. Creative leaders look for the consistency in a person's pattern, but they also look for the inconsistency. A CL is quick to check in with a person who seems to be functioning out of the norm. The change in a person's pattern might be significant, like a sudden outburst of anger, or it might be subtle, like a sad face on an otherwise jovial person. Creative leaders use patterns to assess people, but they also look for patterns to solve problems, create or modify processes, and to determine strategic initiatives.

SECRET #55

ENDURANCE

en·dur·ance \in-ˈduȓ-ən(t)s, -ˈdyuȓ-, en-\

1. the ability to sustain a prolonged stressful effort or activity.
2. the quality of continuing for a long time.

ENDURANCE

A friend of mine was recently telling me about a 43-mile race he would soon be participating in. I told him I thought that would sure be a long bike ride, and he responded by telling me it was an endurance <u>run</u>. He went on to say they call it an <u>extreme marathon</u>. Hey, call me stupid, but I thought all marathons were *extreme*.

After we went our separate ways, I couldn't help but wonder how a person runs 43 consecutive miles. So, I did a little research, and I found out that endurance has a lot more to do with a person's *will* than it does their body. Sure, it takes a lot of physical conditioning to run that far, but even the most physically fit people aren't able to take their high level of fitness and somehow power it with their mind to produce that kind of endurance. On the other hand, people with superior willpower somehow convince themselves to press on through impossible circumstances—the kind in which others quit.

Did you know that most elite military groups like the Navy Seals initially focus more on a recruit's mental endurance than they do on his physical capabilities? In fact, the Seals actively recruit successful athletes simply because they have an uncommon capacity for mental endurance—a trait the Seals heavily rely on.

SECRET #55 to Creative Leadership:
Creative leaders know that everything they do should not be approached at sprint-level speed. Sure, there are times when there is need to sprint to produce an outcome, but that should not be the norm—much of what leaders do requires a slow, steady, marathon-like approach. CLs know that during the slower-paced marathon projects, there is a good chance for team members to wander, chasing after *shiny balls*. They know people can lose interest and want to jump to other tasks. Focusing during lengthy projects is part of <u>endurance</u>.

SECRET #56

INTERPERSONAL

in·ter·per·son·al   \-ˈpərs-nəl\

1. Of or pertaining to the relations between persons.

INTERPERSONAL

I've studied human behavior for a little more than two decades, so very little surprises me when it comes to people's mannerisms. Having said that, I AM, however, <u>very</u> surprised at how overt and direct some individuals are when they interact with others—they simply don't hold back; they just say what's on their minds.

This was perfectly illustrated when I was working with some junior executives at a well-known broadcast media company. One of the HR generalists told me that a particular executive simply refused to interact with people in the mornings. He would point-blank tell his employees, "I don't *do* people until 11am, so come back then." Shocking, right?

There was nothing hidden, subtle, or soft about his message. Little did he know, that many years later, he would serve as the *what-not-to-do* example on interpersonal skills in this book.

If you want to increase your chances of success in this world, you are going to need to be more centered on others than on yourself. Just like an <u>Inter</u>state is a road connecting one state to another, <u>inter</u>personal skills connect one person to another. We need each other. Our lives were meant to be lived together and intertwined with one another. Trampling on people doesn't serve any useful purpose, and it will only have an eventual kickback on the person doing the trampling. "Do unto others as you would have them do unto you."

SECRET #56 to Creative Leadership:
Creative leaders love people. They love to connect with and interact with all kinds of people because it is from those connections that true synergy can be sourced and harnessed. CLs are experts at bringing people together and weaving their singular contributions into one amazing masterpiece.

113

SECRET #57

LOYALTY

loy·al \ˈlȯi(-ə)l\
1. unswerving in allegiance.

LOYALTY

One of the world's most fascinating places is the Tower of London, located by the river Thames in the very center of London, England. To this day, the Tower is secured by colorfully dressed guards officially named Yeoman Warders but more widely known by their "Beefeater" nickname since they were once paid in chunks of beef when it was a very rare commodity.

Initially used as a royal residence, the Tower became a fearsome prison and torture chamber whose famous inhabitants included: Anne Boleyn, Sir Walter Raleigh and Lady Jane Grey. They, among others, were jailed simply because the King decided their allegiance to him was not everything he demanded.

As foolish as that may sound, I've come across a lot of corporate leaders who seem to have taken a page out of the royal dictator's playbook. They *rule* through a fear-based approach, creating a completely false sense of loyalty in their "subjects"—a.k.a. employees. Fearful compliance should never be confused with loyalty.

SECRET #57 to Creative Leadership:
Your team members are not dogs—they don't have an instant sense of loyalty just because you have been assigned as their leader. They may initially follow you because of the *position you hold*, and they are required to do so, but their loyalty to you is actually created through the care, concern and compassion you demonstrate for them each and every day. A CL creates loyalty by <u>being</u> loyal. CLs devote themselves to their employees with unswerving allegiance, and along the way, they see the same allegiance returned to them. Loyalty grows in an environment filled with mutual respect and trust. Creative leaders willingly extend trust because they believe in the goodness of people. CLs are willing to risk betrayal—the reward is worth the risk.

SECRET #58

REPETITION

rep·e·ti·tion \ˌre-pə-ˈti-shən\

1. the act of saying or doing something again; the act of repeating something.

REPETITION

"Tis a lesson you should heed, try, try again. If at first you don't succeed, try, try again."

This oft used proverb has been traced back to 1840 and is attributed to American educator Thomas H. Palmer in his authored work *Teacher's Manual*. The message? Don't give up. Repetition is the key to the mastery you seek.

My dad was big on repetition—that's partly why he was so successful. Whether it involved multiplication tables, golf swings, or paper collating projects in the basement of our Chicago home, Dad always proved repetition would lead to a high level of mastery.

I still marvel at how he did certain things. For example, even when he was 75 years old, he was still faster than the grocery store clerk at coming up with the after-tax total for an entire basket of groceries. The clerk scanned it all using a computer—Dad, however, added it all up in his head. As Ripley would say: "Believe It or Not." Trust me, you should believe it. There was one very good reason for my Dad's amazing abilities, and that is repetition. Got it wrong this time? Just keep doing it again and again and again— eventually, you will get it right—again and again and again.

SECRET #58 to Creative Leadership:
If you have been leading for any length of time, you have probably figured out by now that people don't always get things right the first time. One of a leader's greatest strengths is his willingness to wait for results. Creative leaders extend grace when everything inside of them screams for discipline and results. On the path to great results, creative leaders know that failure is inevitable. They encourage the second, third, and fourth efforts of their employees. They insist on repetition as it builds character, it forces forward progress, and it teaches the power of perseverance. Repetition takes unfamiliar things and makes them familiar.

117

SECRET #59

ENERGY

en·er·gy \'e-nər-jē\

1. ability to be active; the physical or mental strength that allows you to do things.
2. the capacity of acting or being active.

ENERGY

Juan Valdez may not be a real person, but I still think he's someone special. For without Valdez, I may never have known of the tantalizing aroma and smooth succulent flavors of the Columbian coffee bean. For without it, I would have no energy whatsoever. Well, at least that's what my brain tells me.

You know what my brain should really be telling me? "I'm 80% water, and unless you hydrate me with a minimum of 64 ounces of water daily, you can drink an ocean of coffee, and you'll still be a dead head. Oh, and the same is true of energy drinks."

We are living in a day and time when everything is demanded quickly. Remember when the internet was accessed through dial up, and it took up to 10 minutes just to see if *you've got mail*? Now, if we can't get our email on one click via our phones while we're eating breakfast and getting dressed, we get agitated.

The *need for speed* has invaded our lives to the point even Maverick from *Top Gun* would tell us to slow down. Speed is also perhaps the greatest contributor to this generation being the most medicated, overweight, addicted adult cohort in human history. We need to slow down—expend energy wisely.

SECRET #59 to Creative Leadership:
Creative leaders push people to greatness, but they never push them too hard. If the energy drink and coffee cups are piling up, the energy people are expending is to their detriment, and it won't be successful for you or them in the long run. Burning the candle at both ends may bring the appearance of more energy (light) at one time, but it also burns the candle twice as fast, so it is no longer useful in a much shorter period of time. CLs think about creating a slow, sustainable burn. They bring more "candles" and use them all evenly.

119

SECRET #60

POWER

pow·er \'pau̇(-ə)r\

1. legal or official authority, capacity, or right.
2. the ability or right to control people or things.
3. physical might.

POWER

The President of the United States is often referred to as the most powerful man in the world, and while there is no dispute about the commanding voice our President has on the national stage, I can't help but wonder what we really mean by *power*. After all, most of our presidents have greatly struggled to balance our budget, to get the members of our Congress to work together, or even to unite our nation's citizens. That doesn't sound like the mark of a powerful person, does it?

Well, one thing our presidents have taught us for sure is that even those with the fanciest titles and loftiest positions still have limited power if they don't have the support of their people. As it turns out, power and loyalty have a very strong connection, and the value gained by their unity has an incalculable synergy which would be inadvisable to overlook.

SECRET #60 to Creative Leadership:
Creative leaders don't coercively muscle people into doing their bidding because it isn't an effective use of power. CLs know the best use of power is by influence, not coercion. With an influential approach, you get people to willing do things by your mere suggestion simply because they believe in you and trust you. Conversely, if you use coercion, people will likely follow you, but they will also resent you for it, and they will look for opportunities to let your plans fail. They won't have your back, even if it temporarily appears that they do. So many people these days lead with fear tactics and intimidation, and their leadership is so obviously not respected. Even the greatest military generals don't lead with fear. There is power in what you do and what you don't do. There is also power in what you say and what you don't say. And perhaps most importantly, there is massive power in what you <u>tell</u> others to do but <u>WON'T</u> do yourself.

SECRET #61

CARE

care \ˈker\

1. effort made to do something correctly, safely, or without causing damage.
2. things that are done to keep something in good condition.
3. a disquieted state of mixed uncertainty, apprehension, and responsibility.

CARE

Being a parent is one of the toughest roles a person will ever fill, especially because of the *caring* nature associated with it. There are times when your kids are making all the wrong decisions, and it eats you up on the inside. In those moments, you can find yourself saying you don't care, but you know you do—you can't help but care.

It's funny, but pretending not to care is something we all seem to do really well. I think it serves as an insulator for our emotions. I also think we do this because when we care we accept a certain amount of responsibility for the outcomes that await us.

Consider the last time you asked a friend where he wanted to eat lunch, and you heard in reply, "I don't care, anywhere." Was that his honest response? Doubtful. In fact, it probably became evident that he *did* care as you made one suggestion after another only to see them all shot down.

You see, if your friend came right out and showed you he cared by suggesting a restaurant, he risked being responsible if the experience at that restaurant wasn't a good one. We pretend not to care so we can preserve our ability to blame.

SECRET #61 to Creative Leadership:
Creative leaders live on the edge and must have thick skin to be able to absorb all of the criticism they receive as they take necessary risks in order to achieve big results. But CLs are mindful that thick skin can lead to a cold heart if they are not careful. CLs watch out for this, and they seek to balance themselves. Just like the projects on which they take risks, CLs know that caring for their employees does involve risk and uncertainty too. Sometimes employees feel you have a hidden agenda when you lead them with care—they feel that as a result of being led by others who did hide their agendas. Be different. Lead differently. Stay consistent, and your care for them will pay off. Make the investment in them.

SECRET #62

PERSISTENCE

per·sis·tence \pər-ˈsis-tən(t)s, -ˈzis-\

1. the state of occurring or existing beyond the usual, expected, or normal time.

PERSISTENCE

In September of 2013, Diana Nyad became the first person to swim the 110 miles from Havana, Cuba to Key West, Florida unassisted and without the benefit of a shark cage. The fact that she did it is amazing enough, but *how* she got to that point is even more unbelievable.

Nyad had a dream 35 years earlier about making that swim, and at the age of 29, she tried and failed. She would go on to try it three more times over the next three decades, and each time she was stopped by either exhaustion, poisonous jellyfish stings, or in one case, an 11-hour long asthma attack. But she persisted.

Finally, at the age of 64, she overcame unthinkable odds and lived out her dream. Nyad never gave up. Despite the memory of previous painful, unsuccessful attempts, she got back in the water and tried again. At one point in her journey, she was so exhausted, she began to audibly sing lullabies to herself loudly enough for her medical crew to hear her from a boat nearby. She swam for nearly 53 hours straight.

SECRET #62 to Creative Leadership:
We all have to fight the voice in our heads that tells us to give up when things get tough. You absolutely must find a way to persist. Remember, ordinary efforts typically don't produce the extraordinary results you want. You must find a way under, over, around, or through that wall. If you look back on your life over the last few years, jot down all of the things you started but didn't finish. What walls did you hit that stopped your forward progress and led you to give up? Did you know everyone hits those same walls? Everyone runs into difficulty, but the ones who are successful are the ones who tell themselves that they CAN and they WILL overcome this current barrier. CLs won't let their employees quit on themselves. They inspire them, they stand by them, and they walk with them through those difficult moments.

SECRET #63

STRENGTH

strength \\'streŋ(k)th, 'stren(t)th\\

1. the ability to resist being moved or broken by a force.
2. the quality that allows someone to deal with problems in a determined and effective way.

STRENGTH

Most people are fascinated by demonstrated feats of strength because the average person can't even come close to doing what some athletes have found a way to accomplish.

World record weight-lifting dates back to 1898 when George Hackenschmidt bench pressed 361 lbs. to gain the title of World's Strongest Man. While that was certainly an impressive accomplishment, Hackenschmidt's record is laughable by Ryan Kennelly's standards. In 2008, Kennelly set a new bench press record with a lift of 1,075 lbs.

While it would be very difficult not to be impressed by such a feat of strength, most people are even more impressed by the strength of a person's character and of their personal resolve than they are by their muscles. Dr. Martin Luther King, Jr. was a picture of strength in his life and career. Jailed more than 30 times for insisting on civil rights for black Americans, King put his cause before himself. Even up to the day of his assassination, he was unshakable in the pursuit of his *dream*. As a result of his tireless show of strength, he earned the Nobel Prize. To me, Martin Luther King's accomplishments far outweigh Kennelly's.

SECRET #63 to Creative Leadership:
King passionately sought to create a world in which people would judge one another not by the color of their skin but by the content of their character. Sadly, I think King's <u>dream</u> has not yet fully materialized. Every single day, people inaccurately <u>evaluate</u> each other. Creative leaders know the natural inclination of a person's heart is to make character assessments based on non-character things, so she focuses her thoughts on the good in people long before ever seeking out the not so good. She knows she will find in people what she allows herself to believe about them. If she looks to find integrity, somehow that's what she'll discover. If she looks to find laziness and apathy, she'll somehow find that too.

SECRET #64

RESPECT

re·spect   \ri-'spekt\

1. an act of giving particular attention.
2. a particular way of thinking about or looking at something.
3. a feeling of admiring someone or something that is good, valuable, important, etc.

RESPECT

The popular song R.E.S.P.E.C.T. was originally released by Otis Redding in 1965, but apparently, it wasn't very good, and it didn't bring Redding the *respect* for which he hoped. Interestingly, just two short years later, 25-year old Aretha Franklin signed with Atlantic Records and released her own version of *Respect* which introduced her to the world and became the signature song of her wildly successful career.

It has been widely suggested that men are the ones who really need respect from the people in their lives, and women, on the other hand, need more love than respect—but that simply isn't true. Everyone needs both, and depending on the circumstances at the moment, one of those needs might present itself as stronger than the other. What man doesn't need love in his life. What woman is okay with being disrespected? The *math* on that just doesn't add up.

I can't help but wonder though if the great desire to be respected isn't the very reason people aren't respected. Maybe we're trying too hard for something that will naturally come when we are doing the right things. Pushing to be respected usually has the opposite effect.

SECRET #64 to Creative Leadership:
In order to get respect from people, you need to model the behaviors of people who are already respected. Creative leaders seek out a handful of mentors to serve as their life guides. They study them; they listen to them; they learn from them. A creative leader remembers to regularly tap into the wise counsel of these mentors whenever he encounters things which are unfamiliar. The humility it takes to admit that you don't have all the answers is the very thing which accelerates a CL to a position of respect. When a CL models a constant state of openness to learn new things, he is setting the stage for his proteges to do the same.

129

SECRET #65

DIVERGENCE

di·ver·gent \-jənt\

1. differing from each other or from a standard.

DIVERGENCE

Ever want to slap someone who seems to always play devil's advocate and perpetually comes across as a glass-half-empty type of person? Yeah, me too.

One person in particular comes to my mind. I'll call him Pete. When I first met Pete, he seemed like a level-headed guy whose opposing thoughts stretched our team to consider all possibilities. Initially, he was viewed as a valuable asset—but that quickly changed. After spending some time with him, I learned that opposing the prevailing thought on the table—no matter how good it was—was his *modus operandi*...his M.O. He had to do it.

Pete, it seemed, would oppose people just to annoy them. In fact, I'm pretty confident, if someone pointed the way to a sure-fire multi-million dollar, can't-lose-situation, Pete would come up with reasons why making money so quickly would be detrimental to the company.

Yes, companies do need divergent thinkers who won't sit back and agree with everything they hear, but opposition should have support to it at some point if it makes sense.

When it comes to divergent thinking, too much of it can paralyze us and prevent forward progress, and too little of it have us agreeing to any harebrained idea just for the sake of collaboration. It requires balance.

SECRET #65 to Creative Leadership:
Creative leaders are uncomfortable in environments where everyone agrees with everything. A lack of divergent thinking can make a CL want to scream because a team of "yes" people will tend to produce a lot of mediocre work. It's the pushback which stretches the thinking and expands the boundaries of what is possible. CLs hire people who can take a team's thinking and stretch it without breaking it. CLs won't accept safe ideas which can escape the scrutiny of the divergent thinker because those ideas won't be good enough.

SECRET #66

DYNAMIC

dy·nam·ic \dī-ˈna-mik\

1. marked by continuous usually productive activity or change.
2. an underlying cause of change or growth.
3. marked by energy or forcefulness.
4. the way two or more people behave with each other.

DYNAMIC

Niagara Falls.

There are many wonders of our world, and these Falls are definitely one of them. They are both indescribably beautiful and dynamic.

To put it in perspective, one portion of the three distinct sections of the falls sees a volume of 600,000 US gallons of water per second going over its banks and crashing into the rocks below. Yes, that's every *second*. Consider the extreme power and force of that water. The sight of it is breathtaking, but it is also a bit scary at the same time. Imagine getting caught in the current and going over those falls. Well, some people don't have to imagine it because they intentionally take on the falls just to see if they can survive an encounter with them. Unfortunately, most of them die.

The first person to survive the plunge was a 63-year old female schoolteacher named Annie Edson Taylor. Annie did her stunt in 1901 expecting fame and fortune—that wasn't her outcome. Despite her successful encounter with the falls, her victory wasn't celebrated. She ultimately died in poverty.

Most people are not successful in their attempts because the water is so forceful—and the current is ever-changing. These risk-takers have no idea when or where they will impact the bottom, and once they do, the water often does not release them from its clutches—many die due to lack of oxygen. Others are simply beaten to death by the crushing force of the water.

SECRET #66 to Creative Leadership:
While Niagara is known for destructive powers, its energy is also used for good—hydroelectricity. Creative leaders find ways to shift the dynamics of their surroundings so forces which are powerfully negative can be harnessed and used in ways which are positive and productive. In many cases, the "force" is a person—CLs influence a change in the "flow".

SECRET #67

DELEGATION

del·e·gate \'de-li-gət, -ˌgāt\

1. to give (control, responsibility, authority, etc.) to someone.
2. to trust someone with (a job, duty, etc.)
3. to entrust to another.

DELEGATION

Early on in my corporate career, I learned one very important, long-lasting lesson—almost no one knows how to effectively delegate, so brace for impact.

For some reason, many leaders are of the mind that the delegation of their work is somehow an escape clause for them, so they look around for any poor unsuspecting—and likely untrained—soul on which to dump their undesirable task. As a result, the job often isn't completed on time or up to standard, and the delegator—who is still ultimately responsible for the outcome—looks for a person upon which to pin the blame. Sounds great, doesn't it? Where can I sign up for some of that?

Leaders must reverse this trend. Delegation must be based on skill and trust, and it should involve personal growth and development. When an assignment is turned over to someone, it must be based on the person's ability to complete it, not on their inability to run as fast as their colleagues can away from the delegator. The process of selecting someone for a task must be based on a careful assessment of skills and abilities, other priorities, resources, current workload, and availability. It should never be done as a random tagging.

SECRET #67 to Creative Leadership:
There are great checklists online to help leaders make better delegation decisions. When you delegate well, everyone wins. When you do it badly, everyone loses.

Delegation can be tough, especially when your "baby" is involved. Creative leaders start mentoring their protégés early and often, so they have less to fear when they delegate to them. CLs also know that they MUST delegate—it is not possible for them to do everything on their own. And, if they did, they would deny others an opportunity to grow. Leaders must delegate, but they also must delegate well.

SECRET #68

MOTIVATION

mo·ti·va·tion \ˌmō-tə-ˈvā-shən\

1. a motivating force, stimulus, or influence

MOTIVATION

Rizzoli and Isles...Hill Street Blues...Law and Order. The world loves cop dramas. I believe we are drawn into these shows by the suspense each episode offers as we wonder who really committed the crime. We all play detective throughout each show, and we individually decide who we suspect. Interestingly though, in the end, we are almost   always wrong.

Motive is a fascinating thing. Our minds are wired to try to figure out what made the guilty party do it. Did you know that "motive" and "motivation" come from the same Latin root word "movére" which means "to move"? So, the real question is: What makes people move...or act?

People don't do anything without motivation. I mean nothing. You wouldn't even get out of bed in the morning if you weren't motivated by the need to eat, use the restroom, or pay your bills by going to work. The most difficult thing— as we all find with our cop dramas—is trying to   figure out the motivating factors.

If we would all just take the time to truly understand the people with whom we regularly come in contact, we would be so much better at knowing what makes them tick...and tock, I suppose.

SECRET #68 to Creative Leadership:
It might seem insignificant, but the most important phrase you could ever learn, and embrace, in all of leadership development is: "Know Your People". You need to get to know the assignments they love, the cliques they are in, the hot buttons they have, the strengths they possess, and when they're *on,* and when they're *off.* Creative leaders spend more time on this than they do on any other aspect of leading. In movies, actors learning to play a particular character often ask a director, "What's my motivation?" The people on your team may not ask <u>you</u> that, but they *are* thinking it.

SECRET #69

REJECTION

re·jec·tion \ri-ˈjek-shən\

1. the state of being rejected; shunned

REJECTION

Dennis Rodman gets a lot of press these days for his off-court antics, but many people remember the days when he fiercely defended the basketball goal for the Chicago Bulls and became a seven-time rebounding champion in the NBA. In those days, Rodman, was widely known for rejecting opposing players' shots and for rebounding the ball. It was those two skills that Rodman used to help propel the Bulls to the top.

Unlike Rodman, many of us aren't good at "rejection" or "rebounding". We often feel slam-dunked by our actual or perceived failures, and recovering from them is a long journey back. In some cases, it's a destination never reached.

So many of us long to be accepted and appreciated, and when we aren't, it derails us. In order to break out of the awful feeling of rejection, we need to take a closer look at who we are on the inside. Other people don't define us—we define ourselves. So what if you find out someone is talking bad about you? If YOU are good with YOU, then that person's opinion doesn't really matter, now does it? Perhaps you should take pity on those who try to bring others down.

Children, co-workers, neighbors, siblings. Their rejection of you is only valid if you choose to accept it. So don't.

SECRET #69 to Creative Leadership:
A person who carries a spirit of rejection on himself is easy to spot. As a leader, don't contribute to it by doing anything to make them feel bad about themselves. Creative leaders search for, and emphasize, the good qualities in each person. I'm not suggesting you avoid giving any constructive feedback. I'm merely encouraging you to lean first on the things which build up. As you do so, you'll gain trust, and that will likely give you access to find out the root of the rejection. Once you know that, you can influence more appropriately.

SECRET #70

INNOVATION

in·no·vate   \'i-nə-ˌvāt\

1. the act or process of introducing new ideas, devices, or methods.
2. to do something in a new way.
3. to effect a change.

INNOVATION

Jacob Barnett is a 12-year old young man who is teaching the world about creativity and innovation, and he is doing it with one simple phrase: "You must stop learning and starting *thinking*." The power of these simple words must take root in us if we are to keep up in this extremely fast-paced, highly competitive world.

Barnett is featured in a TEDxTeen video, and in it he shares stories about the value of individual perspective. Through our educational system, Barnett argues, we have been taught to absorb information so we can regurgitate it later on a test—but we don't spend time lost in our own thoughts about the topic. He suggests we stop trying to *learn* about a given field and *become* the field instead.

Sure, there is definitely value in studying the work of others, but at some point we must stop and ponder for ourselves what it all means. It's in those thoughtful moments when we bend and break what we know and transform it into something new and exciting.

This reminds me of when Steve Jobs introduced the iPod to the world—"4,000 songs in your pocket," Jobs would say. Not long before that we were listening to our music with big clunky Walkman devices with a capacity of 10-15 songs. Jobs, took what he had learned, formed his own thoughts, and innovated.

SECRET #70 to Creative Leadership:
You need to make sure your employees feel free to use their imaginations. Be careful not to kill any idea, even if it sounds crazy. *Crazy* can produce greatness. It often does! Also, it is vital to acknowledge the fact that everyone, yes everyone, is creative—most people have just not fully developed their innovative self. As a child, the creativity in each of us is wildly explored, but it is stifled as an adult because we are judged for what we create. You must lead people back to it.

141

SECRET #71

DECISIVENESS

de·ci·sive \di-ˈsī-siv\

1. able to make choices quickly and confidently.

DECISIVENESS

The atomic bombings of Hiroshima and Nagasaki, Japan in World War II killed more than 246,000 men, women and children. In describing his decision to use atomic weapons, then President Harry S. Truman said he did not do so lightly, nor did he make the decision in a vacuum void of dissenting opinions. Even before the weapons were used, he described the atomic bomb saying, "...it was the most terrible thing ever discovered." But he decisively used them anyway.

I'm glad I will never be in a position like Truman where just one of my decisions would have such devastating repercussions for so many people. Nonetheless, I make decisions all the time for myself and my family, and those decisions are often on critical issues with no easy answer. The same is true of you.

Like a baseball player, every pitch results in a swing or a stare, but in both cases a decision is made. Don't get caught staring when you should be swinging.

SECRET #71 to Creative Leadership:
Decisiveness is what employees expect from the person leading them. When they don't see it, they often see weakness instead. People shy away from following weak leaders.

In situations where you find yourself semi-paralyzed from the abundance of great options you have before you, you must decide on a direction—you cannot act on all of them. Chart them out—do a PROs and CONs evaluation. You may want to operate in the gray, but you often have to make black and white decisions. Then, once you've committed yourself to a direction, don't pursue it haphazardly—pour all of your efforts and energy into it. If it doesn't produce the outcome you anticipated, you CAN choose to reevaluate that decision and alter it for something more appropriate. Giving up on a previous course of action is decisive too.

SECRET #72

RESPONSIBILITY

re·spon·si·ble \ri-ˈspän(t)-sə-bəl\

1. liable to be called on to answer; liable to be called to account as the primary cause, motive, or agent.
2. able to choose for oneself between right and wrong.

RESPONSIBILITY

One Sunday afternoon in late July, I went out with friends for a quick bite to eat at a local pizza place in north Phoenix. After scarfing down an extra-large, we walked out to the parking lot to find my new car had been hit on the driver's side rear bumper. Needless to say, I was livid. I looked around and saw no note and no sign of anyone waiting around to confess. As I continued to search for clues to find the culprit, my friend was involved in his own investigation.

Scouting out the security cameras in the stores across from my car, my buddy noticed one was perfectly positioned inside a little tobacco shop. We asked to review the security tape, and sure enough, we watched as someone smashed into my car, sat there for a minute clearly contemplating what to do, and then quickly pulled away leaving the crime scene.

Obviously, this person chose wrong over right. But you know what? I've done the same thing many times in my life. No, I haven't been involved in a hit and run, but I have made many irresponsible choices. We all have made really poor decisions. "Ye without sin, cast the first stone."

Hey, when you're late to work, and you blame it on the traffic, you're being irresponsible. When you gossip about a colleague, snag office supplies for personal use, leave work early, etc.—you're acting irresponsibly.

SECRET #72 to Creative Leadership:

Are you setting a good example for your employees? You won't succeed with a "Do as I say, not as I do" approach. Model the behaviors you expect to see, and you will see them repeated in your team members. People know the difference between right and wrong—we are hard-wired that way. Some people do the right thing just because it's the right thing, but there is a rebellious spirit in all of us that is looking for opportunities to get away with something. Creative leaders know this, and they counter it through positive examples.

SECRET #73

FAIRNESS

fair \'fer\

1. marked by impartiality and honesty; free from self-interest, prejudice, or favoritism.
2. conforming with the established rules.

FAIRNESS

Why is it that one actress can work hard her whole life and not get noticed while another one with no training as an actress gets the break of a lifetime? Why is it that a pastor and his wife can pour out unconditional love and great life teachings into their child only to helplessly sit back and watch him make choices that lead to a life in prison? Why does disease strike one and not another? Simple: Life isn't fair.

Well, you might be thinking, "If life isn't fair, why play by its rules?" The answer: Life only has two uncompromising rules—birth and death, and you can't change them. The rest of the rules are pretty much made up by people.

As a kid, I was picked on. Not fair. As a teen, I was always chosen last by team captains for pick-up games. Not fair. As an adult, I've been rejected more times than I've been accepted. Not fair. But does that give me the right to treat others less fairly? No.

One day your eulogy will be delivered. You should live now in such a way that makes it easy to sum up your life as one of integrity, impartiality and fairness. You get one pass through life—make it count.

SECRET #73 to Creative Leadership:

I know how easy it can be to form favorites from among your employees, but you absolutely must avoid it at all cost. It is toxic to your entire team. Sure, you'll have star players, and it is perfectly fine to have great respect and appreciation for them, but if you are stretching them to grow, they won't be successful all of the time. Are you pushing them and leading them to their greatest potential? That's what all of your team members should get from you. Some are at lower levels of development, and the assignments you give them should reflect that. Give them moments to shine too. Remember, the FAIR thing is not always the EQUAL thing.

SECRET #74

CHANGE

change \ˈchānj\

1. to become different.
2. to make (someone or something) different.
3. to become something else.

CHANGE

Tony Robbins, a self-help author and famous motivational speaker, is an expert on personal and organizational change, and he says the key to change is rooted in rituals.

You see, we are creatures of habit and are controlled by our rituals—some more so than others. We have rituals in our relationships; we have rituals regarding our bodies; we have financial rituals, and so on. Robbins says you must first assess your current rituals—the things you repeat over and over—and ask yourself why you are doing them right now. What level of success are you getting from them? For as Robbins says, "Even if you're doing the right thing but at the wrong time, you get pain."

Most people would love to lose 10-15 pounds but they aren't willing to do the things necessary to make it happen. We are so driven by rituals and routines we so easily fall back into the arms of the very thing that puts us in a choke hold, preventing us from reaching our goals.

The same thing happens to us in our corporate lives. When a new idea is introduced, we always hear someone chime in about how that didn't work at their last company, or about how that won't work here—and that stifles change.

SECRET #74 to Creative Leadership:
Creative leaders make the environment fertile for change. They encourage old habits to yield to new ideas. They ensure every idea has a chance to be fully *baked*. CLs love change— it invigorates them. CLs also know that the need for change can be a ritual too, so they take time to *check in* with themselves to make sure they aren't mixing things up just to mix things up. They act purposefully. CLs also know that change is very uncomfortable for a lot of people—stability is like an anchor for them. They don't like to be moved. A CL takes the time to inform them, listen to them, influence them, and wait on them. CLs don't run people over with change.

SECRET #75

LOVE

love \ˈləv\

1. a feeling of strong or constant affection.
2. warm attachment, enthusiasm, or devotion.

LOVE

"If you want something very, very badly, let it go free. If it comes back to you, it's yours forever. If it doesn't, it was never yours to begin with."

This original quote from Jess Lair's 1969 published work entitled "I Ain't Much Baby—But I'm All I've Got" has been used over the years by people attempting to describe broken relationships—man and woman, parent and child. I personally don't like it because I think it's a quitter's mentality. If you really want something—or someone—why not demonstrate the depth of your desire by relentlessly fighting for them?

If you love your child, and he turns his back on you, why not launch an all-out war for an improved relationship with him? If the love of your life asks for some "time off" from you, why not roll up your sleeves, ask what is not working and commit yourself to strengthening that bond at all cost? We give up too easily. Don't let go until there's no strength left to hang on.

In the 1991 movie *Backdraft*, Bull, played by Kurt Russell dangled precariously on a collapsed walkway holding his unfaithful friend by the fingertips refusing to let him fall into the flames below. "You go, we go," Bull said. Soon thereafter, they both fell to their deaths. True to his word, he never let him go. Even to the point of his own death. That's love.

SECRET #75 to Creative Leadership:
In business, it's easy to quit on things you care about when success doesn't arrive fast enough. We do so because we feel that if failure is coming, we may as well help it show up quickly so we can get the pain over with. You can't give up. Creative leaders don't give up on their underperforming team members—they simply won't quit on them even when those people have quit on themselves. They tirelessly invest themselves in their people until there is no chance of success.

151

SECRET #76

RISK

risk \\'risk\\

1. the possibility that something bad or unpleasant (such as an injury or a loss) will happen.
2. the chance that an investment will lose value.

RISK

Balancing risk and reward is the very foundation of our financial system. If you take big risks, you stand to either gain big or lose big; you take little risks, and the impact is very similar—little risk typically equals little gains/losses.

Entrepreneurs are among the world's biggest risk-takers. Even though the failure rate of entrepreneurs is 85% in the first year alone, they take the risks anyway. Even more shocking is the fact that most entrepreneurs keep trying—failure after failure, business after business—they don't stop until they ultimately achieve success. They risk it all—and lose it all—over and over again until they finally win.

Not everyone is an entrepreneur, but everyone does take risks. We individually decide what our appetite is for what we might be risking and then decide if it is worth it. Some people go all in on financial decisions while others would never take chances with their money. Some risk embarrassment for the sake of fun while others can't stand being the object of attention. Some people even risk their lives. For example, in May of 2012, a Canadian woman lived out her dream of climbing Mt. Everest—sadly, due to exhaustion and oxygen deprivation, she died in her attempt. The very same weekend, a Vancouver man tried it and made it—he says it transformed his life. Both took the risk, but it only paid off for one of them.

So why do people take risks? Well, it seems we all love to receive rewards. But we love a little danger too. Even if we're not personally involved in the risk, we can't help but watch from the sidelines. We love the thrill of victory and the agony of defeat. It's mesmerizing.

SECRET #76 to Creative Leadership:
If you are going to win big, you can't play it safe. Creative leaders take chances, but they know the difference between calculated risks and just plain crazy. They avoid crazy.

SECRET #77

PURPOSE

pur·pose   \ˈpər-pəs\

1. the reason why something is done or used; the aim or intention of something.
2. the aim or goal of a person; what a person is trying to do, become, etc.

PURPOSE

Why was I born? What's my purpose? What's the meaning of life? These are the questions on the minds of millions of people.

As a matter of fact, it's this widespread curiosity about purpose which propelled Rick Warren's book, *The Purpose Driven Life*, to the top of the NY Times bestsellers list where it remained for a record setting 114 weeks.

While Warren's book is very popular with Evangelical Christians due to its biblical focus, it is inarguably a book which can provide answers with which even an atheist might identify. Perhaps the most compelling portion of the book is where Warren raises the issue of mankind being *Made to Last Forever* and that *Life is a Temporary Assignment*. When you think about life with this long-term perspective, that may shed the real light on why we all have a deep desire to know our true purpose. Life's a long haul.

One thing for sure is that Siri, my iPhone assistant, doesn't have a clue. When I asked her about the meaning of life, she said, "All evidence suggests its chocolate."

SECRET #77 to Creative Leadership:
Leaders can't lead without people following them. Your business PURPOSE is those people. It's literally the reason you exist as their leader. As you focus on them, you will soon discover that many of them don't have a good understanding of who they are, what they want, and where they are going in life. Ask the essential questions to get them thinking about it, and carefully listen to their responses. You can help them find their purpose, and when you do, they will become deeply loyal to you for your mentorship. Sure, you might lose an employee or two to other career endeavors as they figure out what they want to aim themselves at, but that must be okay with you. Creative leaders do whatever it takes to grow people and inspire them—even if it means losing them.

SECRET #78

PROACTIVITY

pro·ac·tive \prō-ˈak-tiv\

1. controlling a situation by making things happen or by preparing for possible future problems.
2. acting in anticipation of future problems, needs, or changes.

PROACTIVITY

Remember how your mom would give you good advice too late? You smash your head on an open kitchen cabinet, and she winces for you and tells you in a compassionate and nurturing voice to "Be careful". Oh, thanks mom. I'll remember that right before my next *accident.*

Seriously though, Tim Hawkins, my absolute favorite comedian, does a hilarious sketch on this, and you can find it on YouTube. He laughingly makes the point on the need for us all to be a little more proactive.

What would happen if we conducted business at work with the "good advice too late" approach? Can you imagine the reaction you would get in the aftermath of a totally failed project when one of your co-workers comes out of your bosses office after getting chewed out for a serious error in judgment, and all you offer is: "I knew you were doing it wrong"?

Well, guess what? We actually do this all the time! We routinely console our colleagues in the aftermath of the tough talk they just had with their leader about their sub-par performance, and we give them good advice too late—as if it does any good now. Why didn't we tell them BEFORE it became a problem?

SECRET #78 to Creative Leadership:
One of your core responsibilities is to anticipate the breaking waves before they come crashing down on you or your team. Explore all possible outcomes, and go into each situation with an understanding of what lies ahead—and then solve for those things. You are the *tip of the spear*. You must be a forward thinker. You must consider the interconnectivity of all moving parts and all key contributors. Creative leaders imagine the effect of every cause even before the "cause" has actually been put into play. Think and act. Rinse, repeat.

SECRET #79

EMBRACE

em·brace \im-ˈbrās\

1. to accept (something or someone) readily or gladly.
2. to take in or include as a part, item, or element of a more inclusive whole.

EMBRACE

In 2006, I flew to Atlanta, Georgia to help build the skills of mid-level leaders at a nationwide frozen food distribution company. I arrived early Monday morning, and after setting up, I waited patiently for my assigned group of leaders to arrive. I wasn't prepared for what came next.

Precisely at 9:00 am, the door opened and in filed a group of people who could easily have been mistaken for a Hell's Angels biker gang. Everyone had long hair, long beards, tattoos, chain wallets, and the apparent warmth of an iceberg. I mentally braced for a long week, but that's not what I got.

In the first hours, it became clear that the gruff exterior of these men masked the kind, caring hearts that I quickly saw in each of them. Like sponges, they embraced the content, and day after day returned with examples of how they had already applied it. Soon, they were also embracing *me*— physically. You see, on day one, I had mentioned that some people may just need a hug. The very next day, I vividly remember one person coming up to me and saying, "I had a tough night. I think I need one of them hugs." Thereafter, every one of these hard-working men came up to me day after day asking for hugs, and they went on to nickname me *Huggy Bear*. I went there to teach them, but they ended up teaching me. I learned to never judge a book by its cover; to expect the unexpected; and to embrace each moment *and the people* who are in it with you.

SECRET #79 to Creative Leadership:
You don't have to physically hug someone to embrace them. When you show them acceptance, they *feel* it. Humans long to be accepted. They crave love and respect. Unfortunately, we don't typically think of the workplace as a space where we should take time to demonstrate those things. Creative leaders accept everyone. They accept those who do great work and those who do poor work. They express love and appreciation for everyone. They embrace every moment.

159

SECRET #80

TRUST

trust   \'trəst\

1. assured reliance on the character, ability, strength, or truth of someone or something.
2. to place confidence.

TRUST

$21.2 billion is a huge amount of money, and that's what Bernie Madoff's investment company stole from investors in the largest Ponzi scheme in recorded history. Many people lost a lot—some lost everything.

Ponzi schemes have characteristics of high returns with little to no risk; secretive investments not recognized by the Securities and Exchange Commission—made by brokers who were often unlicensed and unregistered. Everyone impacted by the Madoff scheme should have seen it coming. As mom always used to say, "If it sounds too good to be true, it probably is." And yet, droves of people blindly trusted Madoff anyway and paid a big price.

It's hard these days to know who you can trust because there are so many heartless manipulators among us. When someone says, "Trust me", a warning horn automatically goes off inside my head, and in that moment, I want to do anything but trust him.

Trust has a lot to do with character and track record. You need to look at what history shows you before you place confidence in a person or thing. If you go with blind trust, a Madoff-like outcome could follow.

SECRET #80 to Creative Leadership:
If you are a leader, you should know people won't trust you just because of the title you hold. In fact, your title may make them trust you less at first. Earn their trust and respect by doing what you say you'll do. Trust is hard to earn and easy to lose. And don't take it personally if your employees don't fall all over themselves to line up and place their trust in you the very minute they meet you—it takes time. It's a process. It will eventually happen. Just stay consistent in modeling trustworthy behaviors, and you will "crack that code."

SECRET #81

MODEL

mod·el   \'mä-dᵊl\

1. an example for imitation or emulation.
2. serving as or capable of serving as a pattern.
3. to design (something) so it is similar to something else.

MODEL

In business, people often want to replicate success someone else has enjoyed, so they benchmark it—in other words, they model it. The term *benchmark* got its start in the carpentry world where a craftsman would simply mark a spot on his bench in order to line up and cut multiple boards to the same length.

Imitating or modeling makes a lot of sense. Why reinvent the wheel, right? But what happens when the behavior or thing you are modeling is not really as good as it initially appears to be? Warning: As quickly as you can model success, you can model failure too.

Think about home equity loans. During the housing boom, when we universally amassed false wealth through soaring housing prices, everyone took out home equity loans and bought cars, jet skis, vacation packages, timeshares, etc. Hey, everyone was doing it, so why not? Here's a reason: It wasn't real money, and when housing prices dropped,   everyone was upside down in their mortgages—they owed more than their properties were worth. People modeled what they thought was successful—and it cost them dearly.

SECRET #81 to Creative Leadership:
It's interesting to study what your competitors are doing, but it doesn't make sense to blindly follow them. Even if they are modeling a great product today, by the time you benchmark it, the market may be wanting something else. You need to research, think and create for yourself. *Borrow* <u>some</u> ideas, but be careful about robotically duplicating other   people's work. Creative leaders are quick to adopt what they know is working well for someone else in the marketplace, but they are mega-careful about using more than is sensible. They know they must differentiate between their solutions and others. They build off of other people's work to make their work the best.

SECRET #82

FEAR

fear \\'fir\\

1. to be afraid of
2. to worry about something bad or unpleasant

FEAR

In 1933, in his first inaugural address, President Franklin D. Roosevelt said, "...let me assert my firm belief that the only thing we have to fear is fear itself—nameless, unreasoning, unjustified terror which paralyzes needed efforts to convert retreat into advance."

Roosevelt spoke these words to Americans at the height of the Great Depression when millions were out of work, poverty was on the rise, and the foreign landscape was uncertain at best. People were gripped with fear, and it was the fear, not the situation, which was keeping them from moving forward.

As horrific as school shootings and terrorist attacks are today, the most damage we suffer from those situations is the thought of when and where they will happen again. It's the fear factor terrorists truly seek, not the body count. If they can keep us from living normal lives and ultimately disrupt or damage our economy, they've achieved their objective. Fear has a big impact. For example, as a result of the 9/11 terrorist attacks, the US lost an estimated $606B in tourism.

People fear any loss of control, and that's why many fear flying, horror films, the dark, and the boogeyman. The key is for us to take back control.

SECRET #82 to Creative Leadership:
Creative leaders never lead with fear—they know that fear paralyzes people. For example, if you don't intend to fire someone, don't let him think that's your plan. It will mess with his mind, and the outcomes you get will either miss the mark or won't be sustained for the long haul. Fear has no place at work. *Never* use it! What you SHOULD do is work hard to find out what your employees are afraid of and how it is impacting them. Everyone has fears—some are more obvious than others, but everyone has them. Find out what they are and work to free them from those fears.

165

SECRET #83

DIVERSITY

di·ver·si·ty \də-ˈvər-sə-tē, dī-\

1. the quality or state of having many different forms, types, ideas, etc.
2. the state of having people who are different races or who have different cultures in a group or organization.

DIVERSITY

Can you imagine what life would be life if everyone looked, thought and acted the same way? No doubt we would be living unbelievably boring lives.

You could never surprise anyone with an original thought because they would already be thinking it. You could never start a fashion trend because everyone would already be wearing it. Everyone would agree on everything all the time, so conversations with other people would be like talking to yourself—and as interesting as you are, you would hate it.

Diversity is so important to the proper functioning of our world, and while race seems to immediately come to mind when you mention diversity, it plays only a small part in diversity overall.

We need diversity in products, hobbies, climates, vendors, entertainment, food, etc. For example: What if the only hobby was knitting, the only restaurant was Burger King, and the only vacation spot was Minot, North Dakota? I think you get the picture.

Bottom line: We are all different. We have different tastes, different opinions, and different cultures. In fact, the only real thing that makes us the same is that we're different. Honor it.

SECRET #83 to Creative Leadership:
Does your team look like a clone of you? Sometimes we hire people we think we can connect with only to discover we have no diversity of thought on our team. You won't accomplish much with group-think. Creative leaders hire people who are different than they are and who will likely make things difficult at times. They hire people who will push them in their thinking and who don't see eye to eye with them. CLs don't want to simply disagree—they want to hear other perspectives, and they want to explore everything. To break the status quo you need <u>un</u>common ground.

SECRET #84

EMPHASIS

em·pha·sis \'em(p)-fə-səs\

1. special importance or attention given to something.

EMPHASIS

DO YOU KNOW ANYONE WHO TYPES ALL OF THEIR MESSAGES USING UPPERCASE LETTERS? WHEN YOU RECEIVE THEM, DOESN'T IT FEEL LIKE THE PERSON IS SHOUTING AT YOU? While that is annoying for sure, perhaps even more annoying is the message mostly written in lowercase with words triple-emphasized using ***bold, italics and underlining*** all at the same time. Okay, we get it—it's important information. Unfortunately, when messages are over-emphasized, as above, the communicator risks irritating his or her intended audience. In the end, even the right message can be received wrong.

Inappropriate emphasis can get us into trouble when we're speaking too. All it takes is a little misplaced emphasis on the wrong word.

Take a look at the two exact same sentences below and look at the underlined place of emphasis.

"<u>Toby</u> took her to the prom?"

"Toby took <u>her</u> to the prom?"

See the difference? In the first case, we're surprised Toby was the one that took her, and in the second case we appear appalled that he took *that* girl. Keep in mind, the private thoughts we have in our heads sometimes come out via our unconscious emphasis when we speak.

SECRET #84 to Creative Leadership:
One of the worst things a leader can do is to over-emphasize something. Making a big deal out of a little thing—whether it's good OR bad—is a mistake. Praising insignificant efforts will water down the really great contributions, and focusing too much on unpleasant outcomes or behaviors can leave folks wanting to give up. Creative leaders are mindful about emphasizing—too much or too little. There is a sweet spot, and CLs find it and stay there only as long as is appropriate.

SECRET #85

PERFECTION

per·fec·tion \pər-ˈfek-shən\

1. without fault or defect.
2. saint-like.
3. unparalleled excellence

PERFECTION

Have you ever tried chasing the wind? How did that work out for you? It's really hard to catch something you can't see, isn't it? Striving for perfection can feel much the same way.

A hole in one in golf; 12 strikes in one game of bowling; no one reaching first base against the same pitcher in all nine innings of a game of baseball. These feats are often referred to as being *perfect*, and they are rare. Measuring yourself against them as a standard to achieve will likely lead you to a lifetime of disappointment.

Even those of us who aren't professional athletes can struggle with perfection. It can be found in the inordinate amount of time you spend on a project at work to make it absolutely error-free only to realize that your only real error was wasting so much time striving for perfection on something which didn't require it.

Perfection grips us at home too. Just how fault-free does your child's room need to be before you'll accept it as clean? How clean does the glass patio door need to be before you'll check it off the weekly chore list?

We often strive for perfection because we really dislike being vulnerable. We don't like to be critiqued for not having our *stuff* in order.

SECRET #85 to Creative Leadership:
Holding people to a standard of perfection sets them up for failure, and, of course, mediocrity is a poor expectation to set too. Excellence is the mark at which you should be aiming. Being excellent says "I'm not average or ordinary." It also gives you the freedom to take the weight of perfection off your shoulders. When you don't have such crazy pressure to perform, you and your team members just might find yourselves reaching levels that others can't. The key to success is found in "the fruit." Low-hanging fruit is too easy to grab. Look for "fruit" which is out of reach but attainable.

SECRET #86

DEVELOPMENT

de·vel·op·ment \di-ˈve-ləp-mənt, dē-\

1. the process of becoming more advanced in something.

DEVELOPMENT

The long-awaited news finally came. Unfortunately, it wasn't what I wanted to hear. I didn't get the job. I was devastated and in disbelief. Everyone around me knew I was the most qualified person, and the hiring manager was a good friend and career-long mentor to me. As I digested this outcome, I seethed with anger.

I didn't say anything for a few days so I could give my intensely negative emotions time to soften, and then I set up a meeting with the hiring manager, my friend Bob.

When I sat down with him, he quickly took the wind out of my sails as he gently but firmly told me how much he wanted to give me the job as I was clearly the most qualified candidate. He must have noticed the instant contorting of my eyebrows expressing my continued disbelief as he went on to explain how he simply couldn't afford to lose me from the position I was presently in.

"You haven't taken the time to develop anyone to replace you," he said. "As a leader in your current role, you've hoarded information in an effort to make yourself irreplaceable, and that's exactly what has happened to you."

He was right. I wanted to be irreplaceable, so I made sure my team members didn't know what I knew. I selfishly didn't develop them, and I paid a big price for it. That event was almost 30 years ago, and I've never forgotten it.

SECRET #86 to Creative Leadership:
Developing your employees is a major part of your role. Rather than hoarding information as I did, I'd encourage you to teach them everyone you know—it will likely get you promoted. You see, when you are known to do a great job at developing teams, people in senior level leadership positions take notice, and they position you in more responsible roles so you can have even greater influence. Don't be afraid to give away your knowledge. It is your most valuable tool.

SECRET #87

PRECISION

pre·ci·sion \pri-ˈsi-zhən\

1. an uncompromisingly high degree of accuracy or exactness.

PRECISION

Minimatics, a machining company which specializes in the aerospace industry, can mill pieces of metal to a tolerance of 1/30 of a human hair. Can you even fathom what that might look like? Their level of accuracy is so exact that any less milling and the part would grind or not fit at all, and any more milling would leave the part with a loose and wobbly fit—potentially inviting excessive wear and fracturing.

Precision matters to Minimatics and to its customers. In fact, precision is a big deal in many industries such as healthcare, manufacturing, logistics, big pharma, etc.

Precision isn't easy to pull off. It requires extreme attention to detail, and even then, mistakes can still happen. For example, a ninth-degree karate master was showing off his precision sword wielding skills at a public event a few years back and decided to demonstrate a very difficult move of cutting a cucumber as it laid on his assistant's throat. True to his word, he cut the small vegetable—along with the carotid artery in his trusted assistant's neck. He nearly killed the guy because his precision sword wielding was, well, not precise enough.

SECRET #87 to Creative Leadership:
Unless precision is warranted in what you do, don't make that the standard to achieve. Ask yourself if good enough is good enough. While I'm not suggesting sloppy work, I am advocating for fast and efficient. A common term associated with this level of accuracy is "90% and go!" You're not looking to invest insane amounts of effort to achieve a result no one would even care about. "90% and go" is a standard which can typically be achieved relatively quickly. It's that last 10% which takes so much more time and probably isn't even needed. Creative leaders consciously choose to avoid all of the roadblocks associated with that final 10%.

SECRET #88

RANGE

range \ˈrānj\

1. a series of things which are different but connected.
2. an aggregate body of knowledge possessed by a person.

RANGE

The human voice is a versatile musical instrument which is capable of producing beautiful melodies and mind-numbing harmonies. In fact, a human voice is so powerful, it can even produce emotions, if we let it.

From the lowest notes we can sing to the highest notes we can hit, we all have a vocal range. For the average person it is between one and two octaves. Highly trained singers can reach four octaves, and an extremely rare voice like Mariah Carey's can span a mind-blowing five octave range. But that's nothing to someone like Tim Storms.

Storms, whose vocal range is a record setting 10 octaves, can sing notes so low, the human ear cannot even detect the sound. His range is so vast it is really hard to comprehend.

We all have a range, but as Carey and Storms show us, there is even a range within the range. We're all different. Different capabilities; different skills—and while one person may excel over another in one area, the opposite may be true in a different situation.

SECRET #88 to Creative Leadership:
Your challenge is to find out the range of skills your employees have and align them against work assignments which will produce the greatest possible impact. As you do this, keep in mind people don't always like to do the things at which they are gifted. Consider skill and desire as you match people to projects. Furthermore, just as voice ranges can be increased with practice, so can work skills. Creative leaders find ways to involve people on projects even if they are not highly skilled in the areas it involves. It's the best way to develop people. I'm not saying toss them into the deep end of the pool and expect them to swim. I'm suggesting that they *wade* into the project along with others who know how to navigate the *current* associated with those *waters*.

SECRET #89

ELEMENT

el·e·ment (el'-ə-mənt)

1. the basic principles or components.
2. weather conditions.
3. a situation in which a person is well suited

ELEMENT

Have you ever been in a situation where you felt out of your league? Perhaps it was a blind date you were on, and the person sitting across from you had you feeling out-classed or inadequate. Maybe you were at a conference, and your colleagues all seemed to know more about the field you are in than you do. Regardless of the situation, you surely got the feeling that you weren't comfortable—not in your element. It takes courage to stay in that situation when you would prefer to escape to practically anywhere else. But in moments like these, we tend to grow.

We also refer to being out in adverse weather as being out in the "elements". It's interesting that being out in the cold, or in rain, or in stormy conditions requires a little courage too. Otherwise, people wouldn't go to great lengths to avoid rough weather.

Courage seems to be a defining factor with this word since working *in, around*, or *with* various "elements" requires decisiveness and personal resolve in the midst of uncertainty and risk. And that, my dear Watson, is *element*-ary.

SECRET #89 to Creative Leadership:
Most people feel like a fish out of water when first promoted into a position of leadership—totally out of their element. The fact that we all eventually develop and mature into these new roles is evidence of the courage we expend to grow. Creative leaders know that you risk falling when trying things that others won't. When you fall—and you will fall—get back up. I know this too well. Recently, my 11-year old daughter was right in the middle of a riding lesson—working an Arabian horse to move in and out of a canter to a walk—when suddenly the horse tripped and fell. My daughter held on tightly and got through the scary event and then forced herself to continue to ride. She was afraid but didn't quit.

SECRET #90

RELIABILITY

re·li·able (ree-lī-ə-bull)

1. trusted to do what is necessary.
2. producing the same outcome repeatedly.

RELIABILITY

Given the horrifically low numbers being broadcast about the public's level of satisfaction with its elected Congress, there is no doubt it is failing to deliver what is needed—so you could argue Congress isn't reliable. Having said that, they *are* delivering the same poor results over and over again, so, I suppose you could argue that they are reliable— just reliably bad.

When I first looked at the word *reliable*, my brain was totally focused on the word from a positive perspective. But now, thanks to Congress, I am reminded that reliability can be associated with negative outcomes too.

Remember that first car of yours that kept you at home a lot because it was so well known for breaking down you would often decline to go certain places for fear of getting stranded? Anything, or anyone, that is reliably bad impacts us just as much as the things which are reliably good.

If we're honest with ourselves, we are probably just as messed up as our Congress is—they just happen to have a third of a billion people critiquing their every move. I think we all need to be reminded about the importance of being viewed as reliable in good ways.

SECRET #90 to Creative Leadership:
You may not have millions of people monitoring your leadership, but you too are in the spotlight. What grade would your employees give YOU for reliability? Have you ever taken the time to ask them? Would they consider you reliably good or reliably bad? Would they say that across the entirety of your leadership, or would there be pockets that would stand out as good and bad? Creative leaders know the power of getting this kind of feedback, and they know that though it might be painful to receive, it has immeasurable benefit to their lives. Do you risk getting this feedback?

SECRET #91

STOP

stop   (stahp)

1. to cease activity on something that was already in progress.
2. to block, hinder or make impassable.

STOP

For this word, let's STOP the typical format I've used in this book and try a different approach instead:

Stop treating others badly—follow the golden rule.
Stop giving people fruitcake…no seriously, stop.
Stop ignoring people in need—YOU would want help.
Stop complaining—no one is listening anyway.
Stop blaming others for the things you've done.
Stop using old situations to justify today's behaviors.
Stop manipulating people— they can see right through you.
Stop playing the lottery and invest your money instead.
Stop seeking professional results from weak efforts.
Stop overlooking the creativity around you.
Stop hoarding resources and lend to others.
Stop being so hard on yourself—you are valuable.
Stop giving the devil credit for your bad choices.
Stop gambling—the "house" ALWAYS wins in the end.
Stop saying you'll go to Europe and just go.
Stop holding grudges and forgive someone today.
Stop cutting your grass at 7:00 am on Saturdays.
Stop pretending you don't care—we know you do.
Stop playing a victim and step into the role of victor.
Stop leaving the next person without toilet paper.

SECRET #91 to Creative Leadership:
Stop taking credit for your employee's work.
Stop looking for a promotion—it will find you.
Stop holding others to standards you don't live by.
Stop waiting to be noticed and just go out and crush it.
Stop procrastinating and just finish the blasted thing.
Stop kissing up to people—let your work speak for itself.
Stop looking past your employees and get to know them.
Stop wasting time on things that don't matter.
Stop focusing so much on yourself and invest in your team.

SECRET #92

START

start   (stärt)

1. to initially begin, or attend to, something.
2. the beginning.

START

Since the word STOP on the preceding pages broke away from the format, let's continue with that approach for the word START:

Start accepting responsibility for the things you've done.
Start a project for the social good of it—build soul equity.
Start expecting more from yourself.
Start expecting nothing in return for your good deeds.
Start loving folks for who they are—not what they can do.
Start doing random acts of kindness for complete strangers.
Start <u>saving</u> people not just whales and trees.
Start thanking people for giving you feedback.
Start appreciating the sacrifices others make for you.
Start wearing yoga pants—they're so stretchy!
Start doing your own laundry—it's really not that hard.
Start laughing when you would rather be crying.
Start dancing for no reason—even without music.
Start building a new reputation if yours is tarnished.
Start seeing the things you blow right by every day.
Start a bucket list and complete a few items this year.
Start realizing nobody is perfect—all fall short.
Start sharing your weaknesses—transparency helps.
Start listening more than you talk.
Start tipping as if you were the one living on those tips.
Start living as though you're dying.
Start singing like nobody's listening.

SECRET #92 to Creative Leadership:
Start celebrating failures—it means you took a risk.
Start having more fun at work—you'll likely produce more.
Start investing more in your development as a leader.
Start being nice to someone who isn't nice to you.
Start seeing the good in people BEFORE you notice the bad.
Start pouring into your employees to help them grow!

SECRET #93

SPACE

space   (spās)

1. an empty area.
2. an occupied or unoccupied location.
3. a defined spot or place for available use.

SPACE

"Space: The final frontier. These are the voyages of the Starship Enterprise. Its five-year mission: To explore strange new worlds; seek out new life and new civilization; boldly go where no man has gone before."

These words were spoken at the beginning of most Star Trek episodes and films, and they almost instantly created a love of space adventure that soon turned into a cult-like following. The interesting thing about space exploration is that *space* always seems to be <u>occupied</u> by something or someone. Space, even though we think of it as empty and void, is seldom, if ever, the nothingness we expect to find.

We've even heard of the human brain insultingly referred to as "the space between the ears". And though it's true our gray matter occupies that location in all of us, it is far from accurate to suggest our imaginative muscle is just a space filler. Every architect's blueprints; every painter's canvas; every teacher's lesson plans...they all start out as empty spaces. It's our mental gymnasium that brings them to life.

SECRET #93 to Creative Leadership:
Some employees have been tagged as "a waste of space". You owe it to your organization to coach them up or out. Allowing them to occupy space won't work.

Also, consider the perceived intellectual divide—or space— between creative classes and academic classes in school. Is there more educational value in one over another? Certainly not, yet schools are cutting most creativity-building courses. Those in charge of such a movement could easily be referred to as *Space Cadets*. We MUST always explore that which seems to be unexplored. We must imagine that which has yet to be imagined. We, as leaders, must discover new spaces which lead us to new ideas and new levels of greatness. Avoid the <u>void</u> and find the divine with a creative mind!

SECRET #94

STRESS

stress   (strəs)

1. mental tension brought about by concern, anxiety or worry.
2. physical force or strain which can result in fractures or breaks.

STRESS

On April 28, 1988, Aloha Airlines Flight 243 had an explosive decompression at an altitude of 24,000 feet due to a major structural failure. Approximately 18 feet of the cabin skin and surrounding structure separated from the top of the craft, severely crippling its ability to remain airborne. Even so, the skilled flight crew was able to wrestle the plane to the ground, successfully landing at a nearby airfield.

The National Transportation Safety Board did a thorough evaluation of the severely damaged aircraft and determined the cause of the incident to be an undetected stress fracture. In other words, the metal structure became fatigued from prolonged use and it finally gave out under the stress of the forces involved in flight.

People, like planes, are also subject to forces that seem to stress them, and over time, those forces will occasionally cause a person to reach their maximum level of mental fatigue—they become *over-stressed*. In those moments, their stress might result in an emotional outburst, a fit of crying, or even all-out rage with physical violence.

It is so critical for us to monitor ourselves and others for the stress we have in our lives and be sure it is tended to before an unhealthy incident occurs.

SECRET #94 to Creative Leadership:
Much of the stress employees feel comes from their leaders. Creative leaders know they must monitor employees for signs of stress and get them to <u>slow</u> down before they <u>melt</u> down. No deadline is more important than the people who are working to achieve it. CLs relax deadlines whenever they can, and when they can't, they add more people to a project to avoid frying their employees. There is no reasonable way to eliminate all stress from the workplace, but carefully working at reducing as much of the stress as is possible will serve everyone very well in the long run—the company too.

SECRET #95

INTENTIONALITY

in•ten•tion•al   (in-tən'-shun-uhl)

1. deliberate, planned action.

INTENTIONALITY

When I was a young boy, I thought a lot about electricity and how it worked. One day as I laid on my bed in the attic of our brick bungalow home in Chicago, I wondered what would happen if I put a metal coat hanger across the two prongs of the lamp cord which was partially plugged into the electrical outlet near my bed. Well, it didn't take long to find out. The cord was instantly destroyed, and the power went out to the entire second floor of our home.

When my dad came running to investigate the situation, I told him I threw the hanger across the room, and it must have come in contact with the outlet—but as you now know, I had actually placed the hangar into position like some sort of mad scientist. It wasn't an accident—I was intentional.

I'm not alone. People are intentional about most of their actions, and then often try to classify them as unintentional or accidental. They really meant to do it, but they don't want it to appear as though it was on purpose. Consider all the hurtful comments made to people that were supposedly never meant to hurt their feelings. *Really? That's what you expect us to believe?*

Conversely, people are not nearly intentional enough about the things that really matter—for example: education, career, parenting, giving, love, etc.

SECRET #95 to Creative Leadership:
You must be intentional about caring for your employees and about getting results. *Accidental* leadership won't work. You must have a clear vision, and you must work closely with your team members to pull it off. But remember, having a clear vision doesn't mean you shouldn't intentionally try things other people might avoid or label as stupid or unachievable. It is in those intentional moments, where great, sometimes unintentional, outcomes often occur.

SECRET #96

SURRENDER

sur•ren•der   (sur-rən'-dur)

1. to yield control.
2. to willing cease resistive efforts.

SURRENDER

It was one of the most famous fights in boxing history. Known throughout the world as the *No Más Fight*, the contest between Sugar Ray Leonard and Roberto Duran on November 25, 1980 in the Louisiana Superdome was a clear example of surrender.

In the eighth round of the battle, despite it being a very close contest, Duran simply raised his hands and quit. He said, "No mas" which translated means "No more." He stopped resisting and simply yielded to his opponent.

Pretty much the same thing happened on a wider scale in the Gulf War when the Republican Guard—the most fearsome division of the Iraqi Army—raised their hands in surrender after enduring the relentless carpet bombing of American B-52 bomber aircraft.

While the word "surrender" is more commonly tied to *white flag* wielding moments in war or a *throwing in the towel* gesture in a sports contest, surrender is something we all tend to do on a frequent basis.

Any time we give up in a battle of wits and quit on a conversation, we surrender. When we willingly hand over the television remote to another fussy member of the family, we've surrendered. When we stop fighting against the thoughts in our own minds and give in to the temptation(s) we know we should avoid, we surrender. Acts of surrender can either be good for us or bad—healthy or unhealthy.

SECRET #96 to Creative Leadership:
Surrendering <u>can</u> be a sign of a good leader. Are you willing to give in and endorse someone else's idea over your own if you know it is a better path to take? Are you okay with yielding in a conversation when the outcome is not important, and the dialogue is not healthy? Creative leaders know they don't have to be right all the time. The key is knowing when to yield and when to stand your ground.

SECRET #97

EMPATHY

em•pa•thy   (em'-pə-thee)

1. the attempt to understand someone's situation and/or emotions

EMPATHY

Have you ever witnessed a train wreck? I have. The sounds are unmistakable, and the resulting mayhem is shockingly hard to watch. But not all train wrecks involve actual trains. In fact, one particular *train wreck* I saw took place in the office I shared with another supervisor. It was an example of empathy gone bad.

I sat there quietly as my colleague tried to console one of his employees as she stood there sobbing over the passing of her mother the night before. As a leader, he seemed to be doing everything just right, but then he made a huge error as he *attempted* to empathize with her situation.

"I know what you're going through," he said.

"When did you lose your mother?" she replied.

"My mom is still alive," he returned.

"Oh, I'm sorry. When did your father pass?"

"Dad is still alive too," he offered.

And then *everything* changed. In almost an instant, her tears dried up, and extreme anger overtook her.

"How can you sit there and say you know what I'm going through?" she admonished with great intensity. "YOU still have your parents. You have no idea what I'm feeling!"

Painful lesson. He meant well but executed badly. He should have said, "I can't imagine the pain you must be enduring. I would be devastated if I were in your shoes."

SECRET #97 to Creative Leadership:
Your employees are all going through some things. Don't pretend you know what they feel unless you've been there. Always try to understand, choose your words VERY carefully, and give huge amounts of grace if/when their emotions swing back and forth between logic and irrational. In the   difficult moments of our lives, we've all said things that don't make much sense or isn't representative of how we truly feel. Be a leader who listens and is abundantly patient.

SECRET #98

COACHING

coach (kōtch)

1. someone who develops people through teaching, correction and encouragement.

COACHING

Did you know you are a coach? Yes, unless you're still in diapers, there's a really good chance you are encouraging, correcting or teaching someone around you. We all tend to play the role of coach from time to time, but for some people, it is their primary responsibility. Many are good at it, and many are not. Here are a few defining characteristics of good coaches:

They don't give up on their players. If you screw up they send you back in to try again.
They never execute the plan—the players do.
They model integrity and expect it from their team.
They recognize the skill sets of their players and don't put them in positions destined for failure.
They are master motivators.
They are consistent.
They are excellent communicators.
They are careful with how they give feedback.
They are humble and nurturing.
They can teach what they may not personally be able to do themselves.
They are creative and innovative.
They accept criticism but deflect praise.

SECRET #98 to Creative Leadership:
As a leader, you are expected to be a good coach, and your team is waiting for you to call the *plays*. Keep in mind though that one of your biggest challenges may be in working with team members who've had bad experiences with coaches in the past and might not want to be coached at all. We've all suffered at the hands of a bad coach. CLs are aware of this, and they are very careful to appreciate others even when they themselves are not initially appreciated.

SECRET #99

PRIDE

pride   (prīd)

1. a feeling of overwhelming happiness as a result of a relationship or connection to something perceived as valuable.
2. self-respect taken to the level of conceit.

PRIDE

We tend to think of pride in terms of the good kind and the bad kind. The problem is that even the good kind tends to venture into those *dark* places where destructive outcomes seem to lurk.

I'll prove it. Think about school PRIDE day where everyone gets pumped up on how their school is the best one. Harmless, right? Yes, until that intense pride gets carried into the Friday night football game against long-time rivals, and fist-fights break out between people from opposing schools who don't even know each other. The pride starts out as good but turns to bad pretty quickly. Hey, pride even causes parents to act like fools too.

Every parent's child is the best-looking and the most athletic—well, in the eyes of each parent. They are so proud of their precious offspring. The mom proves it by annoying everyone around as she runs up and down the sidelines screaming at the coach to put her amazing kid in the game. The dad proves it by tackling the loudmouth father of the kid who just leveled his little running back in a great play.

Pride is in the workplace too. It gets to everyone. It starts off as a good feeling on the inside of each of us and then somehow twists us to have feelings that we are better than those around us or are too good to do those *menial tasks* anymore. It takes almost no time at all for pride to shift gears into conceitedness, and when it does, it's ugly.

SECRET #99 to Creative Leadership:
There's a very fine line between tooting the horns of top performers and creating pride-based divisiveness. Always err on the side of careful. Also, creative leaders must watch themselves when it comes to pride because CLs live to come up with amazing ideas which lead to awesome outcomes. When those outcomes happen, it is natural to want to bask in the glory of your creation. It's better to find a new focus.

SECRET #100

AUTHENTICITY

au•then•tic (aw-thən'-tick)

1. the original; or made to mirror the original.
2. genuine.

AUTHENTICITY

When I was visiting the city of Antalya in Turkey, I went gift shopping with a friend at some of the local stores. One little shop we stopped in carried dozens of authentic Rolex watches ranging from $12,500 to somewhere around $40,000—they were extremely beautiful time pieces. We left there and walked about three shops down to find a Rolex knock-off collection with watches going for $150—they were total fakes, but I was blown away at how real they looked compared to the pricey originals I had just seen.

When I inquired about them, I was told that nothing about them was authentic. They were just really good fakes that would breakdown in short order.

If you think about it, those watches pretty much mirror the lives a lot of us lead. We often pretend to be people we aren't in an effort to impress others around us. We try to become chameleons in environments we often don't even like just to fit in and be accepted. We compromise our morals and betray our values as we fake the success we really aren't achieving—we don't let people see who we really are because we fear that we might not be good enough for them.

SECRET #100 to Creative Leadership:
Start an authenticity drive at work. Cut out false praise and anything lacking absolute genuineness. Invite people to expose their weaknesses so they can get help to overcome them. Accept people for who they really are and shut down false representations. When you think about it, everyone has great qualities, and, likewise, everyone has qualities which are less appealing that they may try to hide. Fake people are not fun to be around, so creative leaders must get people to pull off the masks, and in that process, CLs must be careful to accept the authentic person behind it. That person may come with flaws and scars, but you can work with someone who is real.